Leading
Raspberry Jam Visions
Women's Way

An inside track for **women leaders**

by

Terrill Welch

Note for Librarians: a cataloguing record for this book that includes Dewey Decimal Classification and US Library of Congress numbers is available from the Library and Archives of Canada. The complete cataloguing record can be obtained from their online database at: **www.collectionscanada.ca/amicus/index-e.html**

ISBN 1-4120-5961-5

Printed in Victoria, BC, Canada

Printed on paper with minimum 30% recycled fibre. Trafford's print shop runs on "green energy" from solar, wind and other environmentally-friendly power sources.

Offices in Canada, USA, Ireland and UK
This book is published *on-demand* in cooperation with Trafford Publishing.

Book sales for North America and international:	Book sales in Europe:
Trafford Publishing, 6E–2333 Government St.,	Trafford Publishing (UK) Ltd., Enterprise House,
Victoria, BC V8T 4P4	Wistaston Road Business Centre,
CANADA	Wistaston Road, Crewe, Cheshire CW2 7RP
phone 250 383 6864 (toll-free 1 888 232 4444)	UNITED KINGDOM
fax 250 383 6804; email to orders@trafford.com	phone 01270 251 396 (local rate 0845 230 9601)
	facsimile 01270 254 983; orders.uk@trafford.com

Order online at: **trafford.com/05-0862**

10 9 8 7 6 5 4 3 2

About the Cover

The stonework featured on the front cover of *Leading Raspberry Jam Visions: Women's Way* is from a photograph taken May, 2002 by Terrill Welch in Machu Picchu, Peru. The location of this intricate stonework is directly under the Temple of the Sun. Much mystery and speculation surrounds its origins, and the reasons the Incas had for developing and creating this remarkable piece of work. She expects that further explorations and assumptions will continue to be entertained over time. Her fascination is with the vision, integrity, creativity and skill demonstrated in creating the stonework. It is a tangible example of the kind of success that is possible when vision and persistence are applied to a situation. Yet, we are often left in puzzled disbelief around "how" and "why" such magnificent creations exist. We are left both trusting and doubting the results that are visible and evident. These results have withstood time and compel our continued curiosity. She finds that women's way of leading holds the same mystery, speculation, curiosity and magnificence.

Cover and Layout: Kelly Hewkin, IntuitiveGraphicDesign.com

this book is dedicated to

Kristoffer Douglas Welch
and
Josephine Lee Herman

Acknowledgments

I acknowledge with thanks the following editors, Chris Hunter, Monica Kendel and David L. Colussi whose combined talents and commitment have greatly contributed to the integration and clarity of this text. I am deeply appreciative of Writing Coach, S Fuller for challenging me to be bold. A special thanks to Graphic Designer, Kelly Hewkin for her ability to create a presentation that is congruent with the intent of my work.

I acknowledge the contribution of the many women and a few men who I have had the honour and pleasure to work with in many delightfully eclectic capacities. I treasure the numerous discussions held over a walk, meal, tea or other more spirited beverage – as ideas were taste-tested for their quality and richness of flavour. In my experiences as mentoree, mentor, leader, follower, collaborator, executive coach, client, colleague, friend and family member I learned and continue to learn about women's way of leading. Thank you to each and every one of you who will find yourself smiling as you read a passage and remember your part in these contributions.

In addition, I offer heartfelt appreciation for the love and support I received from my partner David – his kind, solid, and steady belief in me allowed me to wrestle my moments of self-doubt down into more realistic sized monsters.

Contents

Contents
Leading Raspberry Jam Visions: Women's Way

ii

Foreword by Jacqueline Baldwin

In the spring of 2004, I had the good fortune to participate in an innovative learning process when Terrill Welch presented her workshop *"Leading With Brilliance: How To Maximize Potential With Vision, Persistence, And Success"*, at the University of Northern British Columbia in Prince George. Drawing upon her exquisitely fine knowledge and understanding of philosophy, history, anthropology, gender studies, psychology, sociology, and a thorough grounding in community justice work, she showed us how to seek an enlightened leadership practice that expresses itself through the accessible language of creativity.

We were invited to learn new ways of perceiving the relationship between success, and our own potential to succeed. Exercises guided us to do this by looking at the world through a wide-angle, holistic lens, and at ourselves by creating an inner dialogue about our passions, energy, and goals.

Her emphasis is on women's leadership. Her faith in women's ability to become effective leaders who meet their personal and professional goals is built on a firm foundation of life experience, common sense, theoretical knowledge, and practicality. Her understanding of women's realities in this new century is grounded not only in her academic work, but also in many years of experience as Senior Policy Analyst and Program Manager for the Ministry of Women's Equality, Director of the Stopping The Violence

Program for the Ministry of Community, Aboriginal and Women's Services, and Program Co-ordinator at the Phoenix Transition Society.

Terrill's personal vision includes her certainty that women possess a unique ability to become effective leaders who can make positive changes in society, and provide valuable contributions to the future of our global community. Her stated career goal is to "facilitate social change for women through action oriented leadership." She has created a program that teaches how to enhance women's influence on family, on community, and thus eventually on our world, by bringing to the process what she calls: "synergistic, fluid intent".

Now, she has published a book about it. Terrill Welch's: *Leading Raspberry Jam Visions: Women's Way* sets out for the reader a fascinating and rewarding journey we can take to acquaint ourselves with the multidimensionality of her thought. Her work questions some of the most basic assumptions about women's space, privileges, rights, agency and identity in the world, and offers intriguing new alternatives.

In her introduction, Terrill writes that her mission is *"to practice and teach gentle/firmness in the act of social change for gender equality. When we are gentle, there is respect for our own and others' authentic humanity. We can acknowledge and accept our imperfections with grace and humility. However, to thrive, gentleness is best held in close accompaniment with a firm, unrelenting expectation for ownership and high accountability. Engaging in dialogue with women about consciously leading with deliberate acts of leadership is a big part of fulfilling that mission."*

She speaks of her own life as one of "abundance and deep appreciation". She is a woman who has enjoyed both urban life and a life lived in somewhat primitive conditions in rural Northern British Columbia, close to the land, working in a market garden and sawmill. These two realities are not contradictory, in fact it is clear that her deep connections with nature, the wilderness, subsistence living, and the necessary resourcefulness and resilience that come from Northern rural life are the very wellsprings of the creativity and abundance for which she expresses such gratitude. This variety in her background has also given her a valuable understanding of how particular experiences can reflect the universal, and of the desirable goal of praxis: the point where theory meets practice.

What she is suggesting in this book is nothing short of a revolution, albeit a benevolent one, against what has constrained women leaders until now. She speaks of demanding a holistic and integrated concept characterized and defined by collaboration, appreciation, abundance, authenticity, and high levels of accountability. In the chapter called *Women's Way Of Leading* she calls on women to creatively "pick up the stitches of our whole selves" rather than continue with a female version of the Alpha leadership model currently at work in corporate culture and other arenas.

"Leading Raspberry Jam Visions: Women's Way" offers women a new vision of themselves, and a kaleidoscopic awareness of the breadth and depth of our own possibilities as leaders. In prose that shows deep respect for narratives rich with metaphor, the author teaches us, accompanies us, guides us on a wildly exciting journey toward the wholeness that can come from the creation of our own best individually designed life. A woman's life that is congruent with her deepest principles and integrities.

Foreword
by Jacqueline Baldwin

Terrill Welch has re-examined the old-fashioned premises on which leadership concepts were constructed, and found them wanting. In their place, she shows us wider horizons to explore in seeking solutions to the struggle for justice and equality, and introduces us to vivid rewards in the emotional, spiritual and physically healthful ways in which life can be lived and enjoyed. Her book is a choreography for women's leadership.

Jacquie Baldwin, Author
"*Threadbare Like Lace*" (Caitlin, 1997) and
"*A Northern Woman*" (Caitlin, 2003)

4

About Jacquie Baldwin

Born and educated in New Zealand, Jacqueline Baldwin spent time in extensive travel before beginning a rural life as an organic farmer in a remote area of the Canadian Rockies, where she raised her children as a single parent. She has won nine literary awards for her poetry, and her book: "Threadbare Like Lace" (Caitlin, 1997) which sold out its first printing in three weeks, is in its sixth printing. Her book "A Northern Woman" (Caitlin, 2003) is now in a second printing. Jacqueline's work appears in journals and anthologies, has been read on CBC radio, and she has done almost three hundred public readings of her work in schools, Colleges and University classes. She has been a presenter and a keynote speaker at academic and social justice conferences and symposia, her biography appears in the "Who's Who of Canadian Women," and in the millennium edition of the "Canadian Who's Who." She is a volunteer for women's health and wellness work in her community, a member of the Canadian Voice of Women for Peace, and has performed in the Eve Ensler stage production of "The Vagina Monologues". Her work and some interviews are published on the web journals "It's Still Winter" and "Reflections On Water." In 2004, Jacqueline established her own publishing company called Smoky River Books in Prince George, British Columbia, where she lives close to her family of three children and two grandchildren.

Introduction

I am a woman behind women – a woman who supports women leaders and is supported by women leaders. My mission is to practice and teach gentle/firmness in the act of social change for gender equality. When we are gentle, there is respect for our own and others' authentic humanity. We can acknowledge and accept our imperfections with grace and humility. However, to thrive, gentleness is best held in close accompaniment with a firm, unrelenting expectation for ownership and high accountability. Engaging in dialogue with women about consciously leading with deliberate acts of leadership, is a big part of fulfilling that mission.

I ask women to embrace immediacy and be purposeful, authentic and accountable for acts of leading. I ask women to appreciate and integrate their holistic spheres of leadership. I have the courage to make this request because I view women's ability to lead as one of the most valuable possibilities for our future as a global community. My vision is that we walk in the sunshine of our soul. I believe that we all have the capacity and ability to live our lives with synergistic, fluid intent. I believe this will happen through our ability to recognize and act on our opportunities to lead. In recognizing these opportunities, we need to go beyond identifying and using our knowledge about our specific historical positioning. Through consideration and reflection about where we have come from and the intricate external and internal environments of our present situation we have access to what I refer to as our "contextual environment". When we apply our knowledge about our contextual environment to a specific act of leadership, we have a particular advantage or leverage in that situation. I often find there is resistance to accessing this knowledge. This is partly due to the level of vulnerability and accountability that results from this level of situational examination and, partly because this level of discovery requires time – time to consider the complexities of the leadership environment and time to consider our own strengths and challenges in that specific environment. These are practical concepts that can transform our leadership in fundamental ways – ways that allow us to shine and will allow our team or organization to shine – long after the light from a single act of leadership has faded.

I bring my work to the specific attention of women leaders rather than leaders in general because the principles and acts of leadership I am addressing appear to be more accessible to women – whether this is to do with our nature or our socialization is irrelevant to our immediate needs. Men, who want to discipline their leadership in the manner I am proposing, are invited to join in the discussion and use the material to support their leadership practice. I know a few precious men who can and do navigate these primarily woman-centered spaces and I welcome their contributions.

Placing authorship within a specific historical context allows readers to consider what might be influencing and impacting a particular perspective. Appropriate and necessary disclosure of personal information requires precise attention to known and possible assumptions and bias. With humble vulnerability, I share the following information – my porcelain white skin is aging gracefully over my forty-six year old body as my long hair turns white much more slowly than I had anticipated. My genetic treasure chest gave me dark chestnut hair which further accents the paleness of my skin. When I first began working in racially and culturally diverse communities, I needed to find ways to acknowledge and accept that due to our societal history and structure, my skin colour gave me an advantage. This was the beginning of my personal quest for ownership and accountability for the relationship between my physical self and an unintentionally acquired social/economic privilege. My long unruly slowly-graying strands often create a mirror image of carefree abandon and waif-like freedom - reminding me that this woman's way of leading has visibly enhanced my quality of life. The beauty industry has received minimal contributions because when I was scouring daily routines for every valuable second – simplicity became a rigorous practice. The early years of high stress have been buffered through the development of clear visions which I then acted on with persistent intent and flexible measures of success.

7

A rural Canadian background has laid a solid foundation for using and maintaining my physical strength, for nurturing creativity, and for successful leadership. There seems to be an uncanny connection between my willingness to step up to leadership opportunities and what might appear as an unrelated muscular confidence. Having full-body abilities are taken seriously in a rural environment because the consequences are severe if for some reason a person is born without this capacity or loses it. Taking feed to farm animals and hiking the fence lines through snow and under-brush obviously require physical strength, but even the simple act of packing in the day's water and firewood requires a higher level of physical ability than it is necessary to have in most North American urban settings. I am blessed with a high level of creativity that includes story-telling, photography, drawing and painting. Again, it was my rural days and evenings that nurtured these creative developments. Those years of externally rather sparse entertainment have helped me establish an environment free of television programming, video games or other mind-gobbling activities. Recognizing and deciding on acts of leading seems to take both qualitative and quantitative time – time which has to come from somewhere. My experience in a variety of leadership positions sustains my current inquiries about what might be important in women's way of leading.

Within the recognition of these multiple influences, the identification of primary "factors" invites unnecessary simplification. The infinite combination of events and characteristics creates broader definitions that represent opportunities far beyond those represented by primary identification. To act within an understanding of our contextual environment is to weave with multiple threads of various qualities, limitations, and abilities; meanwhile the self holds a vision that is forefront in the creation of something synergistic, beyond what is tangible with the sum of each given thread. The leader that acts from this position is aware of and accountable to multiple situated positions. To perform acts of leadership with authenticity and accountability is to name and feel the threads of a textured understanding moving between our fingers.

So what did this mean for a poor woman living in rural northern British Columbia? A woman who struggled to raise her children, alone? A woman who encountered women's conversations that were guided by reference to "my husband"? A woman who faced "pin ups" posted in the lunchroom? A woman who struggled to find quality child care in order to work night shifts, while hearing an irritating buzz of "women should be at home looking after their own children"? A woman who found support from few men in her hostile work environment? A woman who is now asked to present her business case in a thirty-second sound bite? What about vulnerabilities? What about accountability? How can these situations be communicated to allow for understanding, accountability and opportunities to create change?

I allow partially answered questions to drift – unattached yet visible and attributing, as more questions and the same questions form and then are released.

I am challenged by the tension between vulnerability and accountability. For if I as agent disclose my contextual environment, will I be able to sustain my world of small comforts and tolerance that have been hard won? Who else unknowingly or knowingly also becomes vulnerable? Not only the specifics of location are important but also who "acts." Identification of critical positioning carries with it a responsibility to also assess and be accountable for how this knowledge is used. This does not mean that we choose silence or inaction. We engage in risk assessment that can only come from attempts to understand a multiplicity of standpoints (which are learned through the experience of vulnerabilities).

These aspects of my contextual environment support me in our conversation about women's way of leading. I request your presence in this conversation about women being conscious of their contextual environment, so that our applied knowledge can purposefully enhance women's way of leading – a conversation that has gone on before us and will continue long after us. To have a conversation there is an implied dialogue – a give and take of thoughts, positions and analysis. This book is my part in an ongoing conversation we each may choose to be part of.

Breathing life into an idea or concept sometimes requires several written voices. It may be the thick strands of theory driving your inquiry or a reflective musing or possibly a short missive on a subject. Or you may want a sampling of each. I have chosen to weave these voices together into a tapestry of possibilities using theoretical underpinnings, my ongoing thinking and imaginative dialogues.

Feminist theory provides strong strands of structure for our exploration of women's leadership experience. These strands are flexible, and spun with hopeful possibility. Alone they are difficult and somewhat resistant to practical application. Reflection and experience help create a pattern of stitches that can be appreciated during our day-to-day acts of leadership.

The coaching conversations are an invitation to create your own leadership story. The intimacy of dialogue is used as a tool – exploring and enhancing our strategies for dealing with issues facing women leaders. Coach Farfalla and the leadership characters and situations are imaginary. These dialogues and characters are fictional and do not represent or characterize real events. However, the characters may seem familiar because the leadership experiences that are portrayed in these dialogues are so often encountered. In these imaginary conversations, Coach Farfalla rests lightly with her clients at the very edge of their potential – it is her gift for transformation that moves the agenda. *Farfalla* – the Italian word for butterfly – reminds us to demystify leadership in the same way as the realization that a small change in the winds can have a significant weather effect. You have the capacity to create the winds of change, and the Coach Farfalla conversations, told from the perspective of a particular woman leader, support you to do so. Theoretical constructs and practical application weave understanding and experience in a swirl of fine spirals. The dialogues between women leaders and Coach Farfalla are a major tool use to inspire movement in women's way of leading.

> *Success Is about giving the best you have, to you.. FIRST*

Chapter 1

Women's Way Of Leading

Women's way of leading is colourful, defiant and charged with contradictions, complexities and toughness. It is a way of leading that demands a holistic and integrated concept for leadership; leadership that is characterized and defined by collaboration, appreciation, abundance, authenticity and high levels of accountability. It is a way of leading that benefits from emphasizing the contextual environment – which is influenced and shaped by both human will and imagination. Women's way of leading will pick up the stitches of our whole selves, rather than creating a version of alpha female leadership, which is sometimes described as a useful path through corporate culture. I am creating an opportunity for leading that goes beyond a glossy-cardboard-cutout mirage known as Corporate America. Yes this invasive shiny trinket symbolizes a powerful arena, and yet it is *only one arena* for leadership. As a founding principle, we each need to be accountable for our many acts of leadership every day. We are responsible for as many choices as we can mentally and physically be aware of – all day and in each moment. Living purposefully with our ethical and principled assumptions is an exciting, rigorous and fulfilling way to lead with authentic accountability. I am going to grab our hearts, and rigorously bring our backbones into alignment! So that we can find the courage to lead with holistic intention – regardless of the arena.

There is no need to summarize, map or argue a position within the volumes of material available on leadership. We know that leadership can be viewed as a principle, a practice, a position or as a particular competency. So what! I suggest that understanding the particular factors and influences within a specific leadership opportunity will be of most value to the act of leading. We must get inside ourselves to lead. From this position we can understand the specific contextual environment of a proposed act. Leadership requires awareness of and accountability for our individual and collective agency. Everyone has agency at every specific moment in time. We all can and do negotiate how we engage in our surroundings. This does not preclude situations involving power difference. When we reflect on our negotiations and our ability to hold various standpoints at one time, we create a space for leading within and through our differences. I believe it is an important and accessible gift to be purposeful about, conscious of and accountable for how we lead in a variety of environments.

How might women begin to lead within a particular environment? In defining this environment in its largest context, a global snapshot is useful. What do we know about women in a specific global context? The United Nations 2000 Statistical report on the global status of women provides us with the following information:

14

1. Sixty-seven percent of the world's 876 million illiterates are women, and the percentage of illiterates is not expected to decrease significantly in the next twenty years.

2. Birth rates continue to decline in all regions of the world.

3. Births to unmarried women have increased dramatically in developed regions.

4. More people are living alone in the developed regions, and the majority are women.

5. In many countries of the developed regions, more than half of mothers who have children under age three, are employed.

6.   Women remain at the lower end of a segregated labour market, and continue to be concentrated in a few occupations, to hold positions of little or no authority and to receive less pay than men.

7.   Despite calls for gender equality, women are significantly under-represented in Governments, political parties and at the United Nations.

(United Nations: January 2004. Excerpts from *The World's Women 2000: Trends and Statistics*)

In a question-and-answer section on the Womankind Worldwide website, the authors' state: "in no society on earth do women enjoy the same rights, access to resources, or economic opportunities as men. This is not to say that all men are rich, rather to recognize that whether men are rich or poor, women are almost always poorer" (Womankind Worldwide: 2003). We must hold on to the complexity and contradictions, and resist an easy brush cut and ear-lowering approach to our global positioning.

15

In a particular moment of leading, which of those observations about women's global positioning presents information crucial to our considerations? Which factors can we leave vague and uneasy just inside our peripheral vision? We also need to ask ourselves what else might be missing. We must wade into the muck of uncertainty, and guess.

In the spring of 2004, I was contacted by students at a women's college in Dubai, United Arab Emirates, to comment on women's leadership. I had just been reading an executive interview by Peter J. Cooper about

Sheikha Lubna – the Chief Executive Officer of Tejari. In less than three years, Sheikha Lubna has positioned Tejari as one of the most successful e-market places in the Middle East (Cooper: April 15, 2003. AME INFO FN Middle East Finance and Economy). I became curious about the specific conditions for women in the United Arab Emirates and in my research came across an article in *Choices*, published in September 2003 by the United Nations Development Programme. Though the country was far away, and the historical and immediate context touted many differences - the comments in the article seemed familiar. Two comments that particularly stood out were:

> "It is not that women are passed over for promotion," says a committee member of the Dubai Businesswomen's Association, "they are never considered. If that is not a glass ceiling, I don't know what it is."

16

The UAE-based media has been keen to highlight the promotion of women executives in recent months, publishing feel-good profiles of successful, female professionals. But while individual success stories do exist, they still remain the exception rather than the rule. (Taifour, Majed G: September 2003)

After some discussion about their request from Dubai, I provided an answer that I believe is as equally applicable to Canada as it is to the Arab world. I believe that women have some unique and valuable abilities that they are already using in their day-to-day leadership practices. These abilities provide the leadership strengths that we need as a global community to create a better world for everyone. I have found that women all over the world have a high capacity for networking and sharing information (a perfect example being the email request from far-off Dubai, from a woman in a time zone 12 hours away). Women in general seem to have a superior ability, or at least a stronger desire, to build and strengthen their efforts in leadership using collaboration and influence, rather than being directive and punitive. The women leaders I work with are highly skilled in appreciative, authentic and ethical leadership. These women have embraced a social return on investment (SROI) along with a financial return on investment (ROI). Women leaders I am working with have senior leadership positions in many sectors: the private (business), public (government), non-profit (agencies funded by government and/or fund-raising to serve their community), volunteer (church, member association) and political (politicians) sectors. I draw from my experiences from working with these women, and also from my experience in leadership positions working with both male and female leaders.

When thinking about advancing women's leadership opportunities, I often imagine two approaches both happening at the same time.

The first approach is to work with the dominant male society in creating opportunities for women to have access to and influence on leadership positions. This is a continuing, purposeful, and pervasive effort. Recognizing and enhancing women's leadership needs to be part of our conversations with our families, our friends and our communities. Strategies and possible solutions for the advancement of women continue to be an issue for political policy development. Creating change and opportunity can also happen by gathering the stories and successes of women, such as the article I referenced about Sheikha Lubna. We just need to recognize that what is possible may not yet be the norm.

Our work towards women's equality needs to be persistent and sustainable. In British Columbia, Canada, with the 2001 change in government, we lost our Ministry of Women's Equality and significant public funding to support the advancement of women in our province. Although women continue fighting for women's equality, and continue trying to show our leaders the value of supporting equality for women, much ground has been lost. This is the reason that our work must have sustainability. Around the world we seem to have a continual ebb and flow of success in women's equality. For example in 2004, Brazil introduced universal guaranteed income (US Basic Income Guarantee Newsletter: 2004); in that same year British Columbia, Canada, is reducing substantive public funding to prevent violence against women – through cuts to funding for women's centres, and cuts to funding for women's access to the legal system. Although the dollar amount of these cuts is a tiny portion of the provincial budget, the resulting impact on women's lives is high - both in our society's physical ability to support women, and in the effect of these cuts on our societal perception about the value of women's lives and contributions to the province.

The second approach occurs when women strategically take the lead, and go ahead and work on creating the world they want to live in, without asking for or requesting permission from the larger male-dominated society. I say "strategically" with deliberation, because this can be dangerous work, and a resulting backlash can cause harm or loss of life – not only for the women moving forward, but also for other women in their community or country.

We must act with as much understanding of the potential consequences as possible, and still have the courage to act when it is strategically worth the risk. We have strength in our community as women to support each other in taking these risks. This second approach will be the predominant landscape of this book.

Whether women are exercising their leadership in the United Arab Emirates, Brazil or Canada, the difference appears to be simply one of degree – we are all on the same continuum of change, where our gains can be shifted and lost as quickly as are the dunes from the winds of a desert storm. We must continue to make new tracks and lean into the winds of resistance. I ask that we acknowledge women who hold political space for each of us. I ask that we acknowledge the tension between our gains and losses. I celebrate Brazil's gain in their recent introduction of universal guaranteed income. I acknowledge the continued tenacity of women's action in British Columbia, Canada (BC Coalition of Women's Centres: 2004) as women raise their voices against:

19

1. 100% cuts in core funding to all 37 BC Women Centres,

2. increasing tuition costs, combined with cuts to BC student grants, which results in crippling debt for single mothers and low-income women pursuing an education,

3. privatization of healthcare and the slashing of jobs pre-dominantly held by women workers; and

4. cuts to welfare and legal aid.

Thus far, the category or construct of "woman" has been left open for speculation. I would now like to bring gendering into view. Judith Butler's logic that "if there is something right in [Simone de] Beauvoir's claim that one is not born but rather becomes a woman, it follows that woman itself is a term in process..." (Butler, 1990, 33) provides an opening for this exploration. If we begin to understand that the construct of woman is also defined within privilege and colonial imperialist/capitalist organization, and defines the limits of what can and cannot be included in our discussion, then we can begin to side step this close-circling of movement. We can begin to overtly and strategically apply women's way of leading.

Even to begin to imagine gender as a more fluid continuum, is to embrace the "messiness" of gender coding that has allowed me to make sense out of my world. I am not ready to let go of the multiple positioning I have constructed for myself as "woman". I am not ready to let go of my positioning as a feminist, working for social change that will improve women's opportunities for agency in their lives. I have nothing to replace this construct of my world view.

Having acknowledged these challenges, I want to push forward and recognize gender coding as a site for making visible the close-circling naturalizing narratives. In destabilizing and deconstructing "woman" I must work from inside because I am inside. The decoding begins by recognizing gender identity, sexuality and "woman" as constructed realities that must be denaturalizing, and understood as constructs that, if accepted without question, can also support present privileges. To articulate a woman's way of leading requires our curiosity about the construct of "woman". Present discussion/analysis seems to bring into question even the usefulness of "woman" as a central point of action. If we hold onto the lengthy continuum and breadth of gender and woman where do we go from here? To know we are part of what we want to change is different than beginning to decode "how" we are part of what we want to change. Accountability comes with knowing. Therefore, if we find a way to make visible and practice our way of leading while recognizing our historical and contextual specificity, then we can be accountable for the breadth of our understanding and actions. How do we gain access to other discussions? The most obvious answer is to engage in discussions (strategically of course). We also might want to assess how these understandings are going to be used.

21

Chapter 1:
Women's Way Of Leading

A Feminist Between Engagements – the dance

I often feel like a feminist between engagements. While investigating the strengths and limitations of my contextual environment, I question feminism's usefulness in my exploration of leadership. If my life's goal is to create social change which will transform power imbalances, I must ask if feminism can provide useful ways of thinking, and acting. For an understanding to be useful it must include opportunities for agency as well as knowing. This is my theoretical and practical challenge. Ideology, accountability, authenticity, and our contextual environment have the potential to feed our creativity and influence our exploration of possibilities. These same aspects may also limit, restrict, or blind us from other crucial discoveries. Therefore, without apology – I am a feminist between engagements.

I begin in a place that may appear to be contradictory. Careful examination of our contextual environment as women and as leaders is a feminist approach. Yet, the examination requires us to question the very ideologies that lead to the development of the approach. Through marketing research that I conducted late in 2002, I discovered that some women believe that using the signifier "feminist," or bearing its sign is a liability. For maximum appeal to women leaders they would prefer that the "f" word have a silent position in our practice of leading – left unnamed and unidentified. With acknowledgment and respect, I choose audaciously to ignore this preference, and liberally smear my conversation about women's way of leading with visible, tangy, dark and seedy feminist analyses and references. To suggest that as a feminist I can step out of my "work" and continue on with my day is somehow absurd. When am I not a feminist? I am a feminist in my thinking, belief system, actions and critique of life and self. To step outside would leave me a stationary stage prop with no way to live as I know it. As a feminist between engagements, I choose to name and hold the tension between feminisms and mainstream constraints and liberations – not as a right positioning but as a necessary accountability.

In an ability to manage the decoding steps of gender, class, race, sexuality, and geography, the intricate dance of representation leaves us in continual rehearsal with rotating choreographers. We each are and must be accountable for taking a turn in creating the steps and movements that not only get feminist understandings into the dance halls of society but decide the shape, capacity or need for such a structure to exist in the first place. Gender, though significant, does not weave through our lives as a single factor. The pattern of self is experienced through an inter-relationship between our gender and such things as skin colour, geographic location, age and social/economic position. These intersections must be acknowledged, and at the same time I am following and weaving a fabric of leadership with specific attention to the pattern that is women's way of leading.

My experience is that feminists, like dancers, push and will themselves through self-owned expectations that may leave them fatigued and crippled. This is where the analogy ends. There are no bookings across the country that allow those who can afford the price of a ticket, to come and view the beauty of feminist theory and practice – commenting on how gracefully, and easily the dance is performed. Feminists are turning inward - outward - and again inward, gazing into the eyes of many partners – they do not dance for the entertainment of others. The costs are too high and the lessons too painful.

Feminists are the dancers that practice in the alley, in front of the bedroom mirror, and when visiting cousins, friends and families. Feminists can be found dancing in kitchens, across hayfields, in trucks, banks, bars, bureaucracies, bakeries, and in the classrooms. Feminists are the dancers that try to get their mothers, aunts and grandmothers to show them their steps. They are the dancers in the washrooms who learn and share their steps with strangers. The shifts between private and public stages are modified through experience.

Feminists are the dancers that come together and risk dancing in the parade of living; around and through, front and back they dance, shifting the direction, order, and purpose of the parade. Other dancers join from the crowds lining the street – no one even knowing these others were there. Not the dancers – nor the crowds. Some step aside, so exhausted they cannot face the parade to survey their collective work. Others are beaten, murdered in mid-step. Women all know it could be them, and still feminists choose to dance.

The parade is long. The dancers are many. They struggle to see the shifts and patterns beyond their view. Warrior dancers are sent ahead, some scrambling up on hills and through the crowds to see where they are going and who is not in the dance, not to condemn but to find ways to invite. Their success requires ongoing steady movement, day after day, year after year and decade after decade. Other warrior dancers continue to challenge the steps and demand revisions. The dance is never complete or perfect or finished and still they dance. The dance is what they know.

Many dancers are needed. Many steps, questions, thoughts and actions are needed. Can the dance be heard by those who cannot see, or by those who are far outside on the fringes of both the dancers and the crowds? Can the dance be written for those that cannot hear? Is the dance accessible to those who step by other means? How will we know what questions have not been asked? Is there a limit to the steps we can dance, and can we dance the steps of many? Who is not dancing, and is there a need to dance? Does everyone need to dance? How do we offer the choice to all? Is it a choice?

26

The question of representation and accessibility haunt my sleep. This is the place where all questions come leaping forward when I cannot find a way to step them into the foreground of broad daylight. In my sleep the questions come… step repeat, step repeat, step repeat… until I am exhausted and still I have little to bring to the dance.

I come, having tried to run up the hill to see where I am and to decide where I am going. I am asking what steps do I still need to learn, who can I learn them from? My hope is that the parade is shifting in a direction that is creating a new way of being in every aspect, leaving no spectators. My fear is that the exceptions are the virtually unidentifiable, mimicking, change agents– who can and will close the street; and that the dancers will be too worn out and exhausted to resist when they find their dance is becoming a forever-tightening circle of imperialist/capitalist ideological controls.

My questions are – if feminist theories and practices are intricately linked, and our dance steps provide fluid movement through and between the two, how do we choreograph at least temporary passages that can be identified, marked, enlarged and possibly repeated? How can we share/shape our collective understanding? How can accessibility from within feminist theories and practices shift the dance to make visible attempts to close-circle our movement? Finally, how do we know if this is what needs to be done and what actions might be missing? How can we be sure that these are the conversations that will accentuate women's ability to lead?

I am exploring answers to these questions by applying my thinking to the practice of creating visions. Visions are created, then acted on with persistent intent, as we reach for defined measures of success.

27

Chapter 1:
A Feminist Between Engagements - the dance

Chapter 2

Raspberry Jam Visions

Finding a useful way to grasp the process and power of creating visions is sometimes challenging. We each have a range of experience from which to draw…

Have your ever picked raspberries for jam? This was a regular summer ritual in my family. I have now decided that my mother's berry picking practices were a perfect way to teach me how to create and actualize my visions. Mom would hand us each a container of a size best suited to our abilities, and head us out the door just after the dew dried, to "fill it up before play". Any whining or sighs were met with "well, if you want raspberry jam for your toast this winter we are going to need a few berries." This vision of her fresh homemade bread with butter and tangy raspberry jam spread liberally over the top was usually enough to silence our complaints. Then she would add "the best thing to do is go get started and it will be over before you know it". (These last words of wisdom will still get me working when my child voice is whining out a litany of excuses.) So off we would go.

Now, our raspberry patch was not the domesticated garden variety, but rather the wild kind, growing up between the windfalls and brush piles at the edge of fields. If you have ever encountered this kind of raspberry picking you know all about the loose logs, some of which are half burnt, and whose soot leave black marks on everything that brushes up against them. You will likely remember how easy it is to fall in a hole while trying to reach the biggest, best berries that are way out of reach, but the only ones you think are worth picking. It is on this part of the raspberry picking I would like to focus our attention. How I eventually learned to pick these jam makers is also how I have learned to actualize my visions most successfully.

For example, each week, I receive one or two calls from others wanting to start a coaching practice. They most often want to know what it is like, how I attract clients, how I knew what I wanted to do, and where I got my training. In order to answer these questions, I would like to take us out to the raspberry patch again.

I have always been a bit of a risk taker, and enjoy lightly swaying in the breeze right at the edge of my abilities. This is how I approached raspberry picking. I would grab my pail, scan the horizon for what looked like a "good patch" and start picking as soon as I reached my destination. Sometimes in my desire to pick berries outside my reach, I would go tumbling down into the bottom of some hole. With the berries from my pail raining down on top of me and into the brush, I would wail out a cry of frustration, claw my way back up to sunlight and set my scratched and soot-streaked body back to picking again.

My siblings each had their own approach. One would be crashing around in the brush picking like a fiend with all sorts of bits of leaves and bugs getting scooped up along with the berries while mowing through to the end goal – one bucket of berries before play. My other sibling would be meandering along the edge of the patch, talking to the family dog and sharing the pickings along the way – one for you, one for me and one for the bucket. The sibling who mowed through the picking process would be the first to leave the patch, but would still be sitting on the front porch cleaning the berries as the rest of us returned. The one who shared with the family dog was usually able to convince me to help "finish up" the top quarter of the bucket so we could walk back together, having a visit along the way. In this warm familiar community way, we worked on our common raspberry jam vision. The results were a full winter's pleasure of wild raspberry jam for our morning toast.

I remember my raspberry jam experiences when I am symbolically falling in a hole and clawing my way out, all scratched and dirty. I remind myself: if I already had everything to reach my vision, I wouldn't be reaching. I remember that this occasional stumbling is not a life-threatening situation, only frustrating and at times embarrassing. I can remember because I have grown, stretched, stumbled and successfully grasped what had appeared impossible, many times since my childhood.

On occasion my mother would join us in our morning picking. She would come wandering out with her pail strapped through an old belt that was slightly longer than what she needed to hold up her pants. As she waded into a patch filled with the biggest, most lush berries fully ripened in the sun – which we had all totally missed, she would gracefully slide one hip slightly to the side so her bucket was securely cradled. Then hand over hand, with the prowess of an Olympic athlete, she picked until her bucket was full. Years of perfection in her method, and care and love for berry picking shined from her full, clean pail of berries. The smile on her face captures the image of rows of jars filled with jam resting on newsprint by the kitchen window. At the same time, she is fully present to the sun on her back and the ripe berries moving swiftly between her fingers. In admiration, I would whisper to myself "some day I am going to be able to pick berries just like that!"

Chapter 2:
Raspberry Jam Visions

Berry picking experiences often come back to me as I am working on a new vision. I remember how in the beginning of actualizing a vision, I will often wind up dumping a half-filled pail of "my best berries," in the course of trying to figure out how to get to those big ones just out of reach. Sometimes I will be focused so hard on the big ones that I squish the ones right in front of me. You might say "why bother going to pick wild raspberries when tame ones will still make jam and are much easier to pick?" The truth is that there really is nothing quite as tangy and delightful as WILD raspberry jam. In working on my latest vision of a thriving Executive Coaching service for women with leadership responsibilities, I can see the similarities between these lush, tangy wild berries and the women I am working with. The ordinary garden variety Chief Executive Officer just does not seem to satisfy my nature. I am much more intrigued and engaged by those leaders that are growing against the corporate grain of societal norms to integrate social values and well-being into their work and organizations. These are the juiciest berries to me, and make the best community jam. For others, they may get the most out of working in a totally different area of coaching. I understand that it might not be the right berry patch or even the right berries for others. That is half the fun. One of my colleagues has a coaching and consulting practice that is focused on working with Dental Professionals – different berries in a different patch! Yet, when I watch the video clip on her website, I know she is working with what are, for her, the richest, tastiest jam makers of all (Anderson: 2003). These differences allow us to trade our wares and have a bit of variety with our toast now and again. Just to be clear, it is not individuals that represent the berries and become jam. It is the coaching process and the end result of the synergy between the coach and the person they are working with, that is the berry we are picking and transforming together.

Finding others that you admire and are champions in your area or approach seems necessary to sustaining long-term visions. When I was considering setting up a coaching practice, I researched other coaches who were interested in the same area as I was. I looked at what they were doing and said to myself "some day I am going to have a coaching practice like that!" One of my favorite mentors is Mary Beth O'Neill. I have had the pleasure of hearing her speak on a teleconference, and have read and reread her book *Executive Coaching with Backbone and Heart: A Systems Approach to Engaging Leaders with Their Challenge.* When I first was introduced to her work I felt as if I had come home. I find that no matter how much I may feel I am stepping onto new ground, there are others who have successfully walked at least part of the path before me. It is this support that allows me to dream of the day when I am gracefully engaged in a coaching process with the shiny jars of experience ready to spread over memories, each held in balance in every ounce of my being.

Whether leading a business, organization, or family jam making, there are elements that seem to repeat themselves in vision development, communication and fulfillment. The first element is to have a clear understanding of the guiding principles or fields of agreement that support the vision. These guiding principles are best developed collaboratively by the core group that will be working on that vision. The raspberry jam vision was supported by a strong set of guiding principles and agreements such as:

1. start with the right combination of individuals and everyone contributes what they can

2. a belief that working together makes things easier

3. a leader models what she believes in

4. an agreement that people are responsible for following through on their part of the overall vision – this is facilitated by developing a clear objective and scope for the project that is well defined and understood (such as a winter supply of wild raspberry jam for our family)

5. a profound team knowledge and set of best practices about the business of homemade jam making.

When we develop a strong set of guiding principles and agreements that a team can verbalize and take ownership for, there is a greater possibility that the vision can be actualized.

I have a strong bias towards collaborative vision building even if you are working as a sole entrepreneur. Often we talk about teams. I prefer to talk about communities, where we consciously recognize a variety of internal and external players; these players come together in synergistic units to successfully achieve different aspects of a vision. We can greatly enhance our possibilities for success by purposefully developing these diverse webs of internal and external patterns. I see community and team as part of the core foundation of any vision. When we are leading and taking overt responsibility for a vision it becomes crucial to ask: who else needs to be part of this conversation? And who else needs to take a leadership role for this to succeed? Collaboration is one of the strengths that women leaders typically bring to their work environment. Often, our life experience as women has necessitated that we practice and perfect collaborative community building. As leaders we can achieve further finesse with these skills, with minimal risk.

To go beyond the creation of our vision there is a necessary element of persistence in the intent behind the vision. We define the goals and create measurable objectives. At the same time we negotiate tasks, timelines and lead responsibilities. With this done, we can then review the planning process against the intent behind the vision. One of the defining differences between a dream and a vision is to decide if it is actionable. A dream is a nice idea and becomes a vision when it has clear actions that someone is prepared to make happen! This is true equally for a short-term project such as picking the wild raspberries for jam, or a long-term project that will take more than a lifetime.

Finally, there needs to be a clear articulation about what success will look, feel and be like when the vision is reached. The more detail that can be developed the stronger the possibility of achieving it. Ask if the vision, goals and objectives are reasonable and if there is high potential for achievement. Ask if the vision reflects a holistic view. For example, in picking raspberries for jam, there was also a clear understanding and commitment to having time to play. A leader and a team need to be prepared to clarify, reflect, reshape and refine visions against goals and objectives. If it rained for 3 weeks in late July and early August our crop of raspberries were significantly diminished. This meant picking more than the usual amount of wild high-bush cranberries to make a sweet jelly (also very good). The underlying intent was to end up with something sweet to put on our toast. Ideally, visions have a degree of flexibility and fluidity rather than becoming hard, fixed and stagnant. When we are working on a vision that is in alignment with our mission and purpose, there is a good chance that the work will be energizing. Measuring the meaningfulness of a vision is often discernable by the degree of pleasure we derive from working on it. Hardly being able to wait to get out of bed in the morning to begin working on something –is a good sign!

Coach Farfalla and Sarah: vision – getting started

Facing our life with frank vulnerability is key to discovering what we are most passionate about. Often, we first need to answer the question about what fills us with vitality and energy. We can then share our vision with others – building internal and external communities – to ensure our success. Sometimes we will move forward swiftly, and other times we will fall pell-mell into a deep dark dirty hole. Each experience and each attempt towards our vision will bring us closer to success. With clarity and persistence, we hold onto the intent behind our vision. Coach Farfalla and Sarah's telephone coaching conversation provides us with one way of approaching our vision work.

In becoming the Chief Executive Officer of a large research centre on women's health, Sarah has reached her most obvious career goal. Sarah is disappointed that it hasn't resulted in the feeling of fulfillment and satisfaction that she has spent many years anticipating. Her work routine is characterized by long hours at the office, too much coffee and too many missed meals and broken commitments with friends and families. Yet, she is doing the work she loves. She has spent much of her career working towards this moment. This overwhelming feeling of believing there must be more – much more – has resulted in Sarah hiring Coach Farfalla. The beginning of their coaching work is having a rather rocky start.

Sarah is writing an email to Farfalla. Sarah cannot believe she is writing a note of apology. She had been looking forward to her first discovery session yesterday. At least, she thought she had been looking forward to the call.

Sarah is aware that there are times when her resistance is passive and she simply forgets. She forgets to get groceries on the way home because cooking is not her thing. She forgets to call her friends back when they want to do things together, because she feels guilty about being unable to see them. She forgets to pick up the forms to fill out for her will, because she doesn't want to decide what to do with her stuff, or to think about dying. Now, she has forgotten her coaching call. After an hour of grating internal self-chastisement, Sarah is apologizing and still wondering why she missed the appointment. She has to decide if she wants to reschedule. If so, when can she fit it in? Her assistant is already working to figure out how to resolve two double bookings this week, and what with travel time to get to three of her meetings, she isn't sure she will even have time for lunch.

Sarah is propping her fried brain on her right hand. With her elbow on the edge of the desk and her shoulders slumped, she frowns out the office window. How did she end up here? What does she really want anyway? It is seven in the morning, and she can feel the cold draft coming from the gap between her desire and the energy she needs to exercise it.

She sends the email to Farfalla, sighs – reaches for the foot-high stack of signing that was due two days ago in finance. There is no time now to decide direction. Sarah thinks out loud, "I just want my brain back. I just want time to think. Is that too much to ask?" There is no answer in the predawn building, lit only by the glow of her desk lamp. Each word becomes an echo, like the dripping of a tap that she cannot turn off.

Over the next couple of days, Sarah and Farfalla are able to schedule and work their way through a 'get to know you' session. During their current coaching telephone call, Farfalla has just asked Sarah what dreams she has given up on. Sarah does not want to answer. Sarah fears if she gives voice to these failed, shrunken desires, her despair will wrap a cloak of invisibility around her shoulders and she will disappear – Vanish! Dissolve! Evaporate!

When was the last time you heard your own desires?

What did you say to yourself?

How do you recognize when you are honoring your needs, rather than avoiding what you do not want to face?

39

Instead Sarah tries a defensive position: "How come other people know what they want and seem to have great lives? They have kids, partners and weekends at the lake. I just can't see how I could get those things to happen. If I even took time for a daily walk, the mass of clutching 'action items' would leave my office a mess and my workload unmanageable. Believe me, I have tried. It doesn't work no matter how many of those best-seller self-help books I read. They can peddle their glitzy 'follow your dreams' one-liners all they want. My life stays pretty much the same. I don't get it. I must really be missing something."

Farfalla catches the breeze of resistance as it passes by, and then she asks softly "If we had a handful of magic and if you could be anywhere in the world, where would you be and who would be there?"

Sarah grumps "I don't want to play."

Farfalla shifts again, gathering the original request that Sarah brought to her and sweeps it gently forward to catch Sarah's attention "When you first called me, I remember your determined comments about wanting to discover and follow your life's purpose. You were persistent about your desire to create a clear vision or direction for yourself, and you wondered if that was part of what coaching could offer. Do you remember that conversation?"

How are your fears about fully living your dreams serving you?

Consider how your resistance to what you want, keeps you where you are today.

"Yes."

"Where is that part of you that had such resolve? Where is that person today?"

Sarah can feel her chest moving in and out as she scrambles to get herself to a place of articulation. Then she relaxes into her fear and the words tumble out.

"What if I can't do this? What if I am incapable of finding a way to be me and live the life I want? I have so much security right now. I have a great job even if it takes up my every waking hour. Besides, I am terrified that there really isn't anything more to life. If I look and see that this is really all there is, how will I have the will to keep working so hard?"

"I believe that our fears have a purpose. What might be the purpose of being 'terrified' that there is no more to life?"

Sarah pauses as the silence is filled with possible answers. Then one answer comes forward and she begins to know. Coach Farfalla and Sarah end the session with Sarah deciding to observe her fear until their call next week.

41

If you had a handful of **magic**, what would your ideal life be?

Sarah has spent significant time over the past week observing how her fear and resistance have been serving her. Her commitment was only to observe – to take no action. So she has been observing how she feels, her body language and her self-talk. Sarah has decided that though her life is full, and by societal measures of money and status, it is successful, she is ready for something more. Her fear of the 'something more' is what has been keeping her treading water in the same routine of work-and-more-work for a number of years. As the Chief Executive Officer of a large research centre on women's health, there is an implicit agreement that her salary is tied to 24-hour availability or an as-long-as-you-can-stand-up commitment to the organization. Sarah accepted this non-verbal arrangement when taking the position five years ago. She understood the CEO culture of 'full commitment'. The seldom spoken rationale is that "yes, I get paid a large salary and I work for it!" Like many women who have moved up through an organization into senior leadership positions, delegating work to others has been her major challenge. She has known this, and can see how it makes her difficult workload monumental. Yet to change her behaviour would be to take risks that somehow she cannot find a way to do. Right now, she is exhausted from both mental and physical fatigue. It does not help to read that large numbers of women, including women in leadership positions, suffer from sleep deprivation. Somehow, knowing others are experiencing the same thing does not ease her soul-deep numbness.

Sarah shifts from her internal dialogue as Farfalla asks "what have you learned from this exercise?"

Sarah answers: "Remember how I said that I felt the purpose of my fear was to keep me safely inside what others describe as success, and you said that this may be true, and then asked how I gave societal expectations the power to define my success?"

"unhum"

"Well, my first idea was just to leap out of my present situation and become a coach like you. You seem to have a life full of balance, personal relationships and meaningful work. That is what I want!"

List examples of how your way of working is both satisfying and self-destructive.

If you want to increase your quality of life and continue to do the work you love, what might move you to action and long-term sustainable change? What has moved you to action and long-term change in the past?

"And what did you learn from your observation?"

"Coaching is how you choose to express your life. It is a perfect fit with your passion, desire and dreams. For me, I just wanted the benefits of your life style. Working with people like me all day is not my idea of fulfillment."

Farfalla laughs and teases "I don't know, I find you perfectly delightful, engaging and honestly self-reflective. Seems like a great way to spend part of my day to me."

43

"My point exactly! What I want is a shift in life style while continuing in my present position. I want to be able to do this job because it continues to be meaningful to me. AND I want to be able to have a life outside of work, including time to think about my personal dreams. I want to stop this one-sided dimensional living, which is 99% work. I even dream about my work. How sick is that?"

Farfalla lets Sarah's last self-admonishment slide by into her mental "bring forward" file for later. Instead she asks "so what do you want to do next?"

Later in the week, Sarah and Farfalla are reviewing Sarah's accomplishments. Sarah left their last coaching call having made a commitment to journal about her vision of an ideal work life, and to determine what she had to offer her ideal organization. She had accepted Farfalla's request to dig deep, to include all aspects that presented themselves (even if they seemed silly), and to bring her findings back to their coaching session this week.

Sarah explains: "You see, my ideal organization would value flexibility and harmony as a desired method of enhancing its strength and outcomes. I have done some research that has concluded this approach can increase productivity, lower sick-leave, and enhance creative responses. My biggest challenge is that I am stuck in an organization with a work-defines-my-value mentality. I don't know how I can change that when the Board of Directors, federal funders, and staff all support this same belief. How can I, just one person, create this kind of shift? Or would it be better to leave and find a situation where these were already the cultural values of the organization? On the other hand, what if I find such a place, and successfully compete for a position, only to find it change! — I know many people and organizations that believe in a healthy work environment, but are unable to maintain it in practice. Maybe the whole thing is too silly for words? If my ideal organization could function successfully, more work environments would be like that, right? Maybe I could research other organizations that have tried to create these shifts, and see how they did it... I don't know, it seems like the whole idea would take way more energy than I have. Funding is shaky as it is, and here I want to take on a major cultural shift that is likely to be met with resistance. Then again, I would love to come in to work in the morning and find people fully engaged in their work; that would allow me to spend the

44

majority of my time charting the organizational course for our continued success. But it just seems impossible! ..."

Tips for choosing a vision

First say "yes!" to your imagination and then ask what needs to happen for this to become part of your reality. Your vision and what you are committing to do will pull irresistibly on your heart strings. If it is not – dream again until your vision brings every cell of your being to attention.

A compelling vision goes beyond our self to a "greater good". There is an assumption in this process that your vision is both good for you and good for the world. Thinking about and defining how your vision serves a "greater good," will give your vision more sustainability.

If you are unable to come up with even a few action steps – dream again until you have something that you can and will make happen. Not all dreams are meant to become visions. When we review our dreams, we may find that some are just dreams and that is okay. Other dreams are visions that have the potential to change our lives and the lives of those around us.

45

Farfalla listens quietly as Sarah continues to present various aspects of her vision, and then squashes them with the sledge hammer of her self doubt. Sarah's fear seems to swing with increasing momentum as she explores and defines how she might be able to lead her current organization into a place of strength, creativity, work, community, and results that excel and build on women's health research.

When Sarah appears ready to collapse from the tension that she has created out of the gap between her current reality and her vision, Farfalla asks: "so, … what if you went ahead and acted as if your vision was achievable without knowing how you were going to make it happen? Could you proceed only on the conviction of your imagination and belief that it is possible to lead your organization into a new way of working – does that create the flexibility and harmony that you desire, for everyone?"

"What if I fail?"

Farfalla responds, "what if you succeed?"

Sarah ponders Farfalla's question. Before ending her coaching session with Farfalla, Sarah makes a commitment to outline some short-term and long-term steps that might move her towards her ideal work environment.

Sarah has spent much of the last few days wrestling the demons of her self doubt. One minute she is buzzing with excitement and possibility. The next minute she can feel knots of fear inside her, strangling her momentum.

Farfalla opens the session with, "where would you like to begin?"

"I would like to review the draft outline I sent you for my next steps… I would be interested in your opinion."

Sarah can hear the rustle of papers as Farfalla finds the document. "I am having a second look" Farfalla replies. Sarah doodles on a piece of paper for what seems like eternity, waiting for Farfalla's response. "I could give you my opinion but, at this time, I am not sure how useful it would be. Would you be willing to take me further into your plan through a series of questions, so that we can both see what is working and not working for you through these next steps?"

Consider that some things in your life resonate with such strength that you "must" do them regardless of obvious adversity. Can you think of time in your life where you succeeded at what appeared impossible at first? How can you apply this success in other situations that fill you with the fear of attempting what seems to be the impossible?

47

Sarah replies in a heavy, flat voice "actually, I was hoping that you would give a "yes" or "no" sign and take some of the pressure off what I am feeling at the moment."

Farfalla reflects on Sarah's response with compassion and intent. "I could do that. What that would do is move our work from coaching to consulting. My hunch is that if you step through your doubts and stay with a coaching approach the results will be greater for you. The tough part about creating visions is seeing how they will work when we put them into action. It is not unlike building a kite and then getting ready to send it up. Sometimes they fly on the first try and sometimes we take them back and forth several times for further modifications. If I were to provide my opinion now it would still only be a set of estimations and calculations that would not ensure your vision will fly as you intend it to. What I would like to do is work with you to see if we can do a thorough review of what we know at this time – so you have the best chance of getting your vision off the ground. I would like to do this by staying with a coaching approach while I stand beside you as you take on full responsibility and commitment for your vision. I trust your ability to assess what aspects of your design and action are solid and what aspects need further work. Plus, I trust your ability to know when elements are beyond your expertise, allowing you to engage others to fill those gaps."

> What would your vision for your work be if you could step through your fear and self doubt?

Farfalla pauses and then continues "are you willing to step into this kind of coaching assessment process with me in reviewing your short and long-term steps towards your vision?"

Sarah thinks for a moment and then teases Farfalla: "have you ever thought of letting anyone off the hook of their own ambition?"

Sarah can hear Farfalla's smile in her voice as she replies "I love to see people shine, and that comes from allowing them to stand in their fullest potential."

Over the next few weeks Sarah works with Farfalla to map out her plans for her vision in relation to Women's Health Research, and what needs to happen in her organization to support this vision. Sarah develops a plan for approaching the Board of Directors, funders, colleagues and staff. She determines what aspects of her vision are up to her to create, and which aspects will require other resources or the commitment and dedication of others to achieve. Sarah is ready to fly her kite with a full team of support to work on any modifications, if and when they are required.

49

Developing initial short-term and long-term steps for your vision

Getting from a dream to a vision requires a plan. There are several methods that can help us to do this, such as guided imagery or a swot (strengths, weaknesses, opportunities and threats) analysis.

Often, guided imagery alone does not have the measurable actions that we need to sustain our momentum. We have clarity about our dream but lack the specifics around what to do next.

On the other hand, going through a linear process of listing strengths, weaknesses, opportunities and threats can result in specific actions but we often lose sight of the intent behind what it was we wanted to accomplish. We tend to lose the fire in our belly and get weighed down under the logistics of implementation.

Developing our vision requires that we revisit our dream and action plans often. Though the frequency of our review may vary, it is important to develop a repeatable process that works for our specific situation.

Another method is called Recipe Rigor.

First, buy a stack of recipe cards in a colour that pleases you, and with pen in hand, block off about thirty minutes of time. Now count out 20 recipe cards. Quickly write out the steps related to your vision. Place each step on a separate recipe card until you have used all 20 recipe cards. Add ten blank or wild cards to the stack for new ideas later. Decide on a time frame that would represent short-term and long-term for your particular vision. Spend about ten minutes each day for a week sorting or shuffling the stack of cards into two piles – a short-term pile and a long-term pile. Arrange each pile of cards from the easiest on the top to the hardest on the bottom. Easiest is not necessarily equivalent to the simple but rather the step you have the most energy for and immediate opportunity to complete. Do this work using your whole self – let go of being right and trust your intuition to give you a reasonable guess. As you are shuffling the cards and new steps come to you, write them down on the blank cards. If you come up with more than ten steps, place the extra steps on a separate list for consideration later.

Next take the top card from each pile (this should be the easiest short-term and long-term steps). On each of the two cards you have chosen, write down under each step, how you will know you are successful if you complete the step on the card. Write down specifically what you are going to do to reach that success, and by when. Include what the intent is behind your action. To increase your commitment and accountability, tell someone what you are going to do and ask if you can check in with them to celebrate when you have completed the action. Short-term steps give us immediate satisfaction and our long-term steps keep us reaching for the bigger picture.

Each week resort the cards into short-term and long-term piles. Always stack them going from easiest on the top to hardest on the bottom. Each week in our life is a bit different and allows for different opportunities. Hence, you may find you stack the cards differently from one week to the next.

As you complete an action and you are satisfied that you have met your measure of success, write the date of completion and place the card on a third pile. Take another blank card and review the list of actions you have saved for later. Add the next action to the new blank card that you find most compelling. Decide which pile it should go on. After a few weeks you may find that something on the list for later can go directly to the completed pile, because when we focus our intent on a vision, some things seem to happen without deliberate planning.

Keep repeating the weekly process until you have either reached your vision or want to choose a new vision.

Chapter 3

Persistence As The Stitches Between Vision And Success

What could knitting and a concept of *persistence* have in common? Well, we could pull out our needles and the three bags of wool from under the bed or the bottom of the closet (likely purchased for some project or other, five or ten years ago) and then see what we can make with it. In developing and articulating a *concept of persistence*, it is much like preparing a conceptual garment design. There will be further discussions and shaping, as the patterns are knit again and again by each of us. My interest in developing such a concept from an everyday word like *persistence*, originates from a continuous litany of questions put to me: how do I appear to get so much accomplished, and how do I successfully "plan" to reach my goals? Why am I always so happy and optimistic that "things will work out as they should?" Am I not nervous about making ten-or-twenty-year life plans – "what if they don't happen?" Or, what is it that allows me to take great risks and change jobs, career directions, and even intimate relationships? I have often been puzzled by these questions and the comments that accompany them, such as "you always seem to know what you want to do" or "you always have a plan" or "you are always so sure of yourself, and confident." These observations are not exactly accurate from a whole variety of perspectives. This is why I am attempting to develop a *concept of persistence* that allows others to join me in dialogue about (to continue my knitting analogy) the choice of stitches that may shape the garment between our visions and success.

Persistence is a favorite word of mine, along with *congruency, authenticity* and *ethical integrity.* The **Shorter** Oxford English Dictionary (emphasis mine) offers an opportunity to identify the recognized meaning of *persistence*. In reference to the root word of *persist*, we can start with the Latin *Per* – "through, by, or by means of". In using the analogy of knitting, the choices of stitches are the "means". The second part of the word comes from *sistere* meaning "to stand". A loose definition of *persistence* may best be articulated as "the action or fact, by means of which we stand" – or "an obstinate continuance in a particular course" of action. Let's dig deeper here and look at the meaning of *obstinate.* The first meaning assigned to *obstinate* is to be "pertinacious in adhering to one's own course; not yielding to argument, persuasion, or entreaty; inflexible, headstrong, self-willed – rarely in neutral or good sense."

It is important to be clear and sharp about the focal point of this concept. What is it that someone practicing a *concept of persistence* is being inflexible, headstrong, self-willed or obstinate about? It is neither a particular vision nor the desired success that we are obstinate about. A *concept of persistence* is about the choice of stitches that are the means by which the vision stands, and the manner through which the vision is linked and shaped into the desired success. Therefore, when choosing to use *persistence* as a method for actualizing our visions we are detached from our anticipated desire and remain focused on our intent, and the means or stitches that best allow us to shape that desire in any specific moment. This stance or intent then allows us maximum flexibility, influence and creative responsiveness. Hence, our vision continues to develop shape and clarity of intent, as the garment of our desire takes shape.

Which "stitches" then should be held with headstrong self-will? The stitches that are the foundational principles we choose in our efforts to move towards our vision. These are the foundational principles we hold up to measure our self-worth late at night or as we look into the mirror and face our own reflection. We need to know that at the end of a day, we have lived up to our chosen principles to the best of our ability at that particular moment in time. We are obstinate and inflexible about our commitment to this ritual of self-assessment.

Our chosen principles, and the skill with which we can assess, strengthen and use these principles, are the stitches of *persistence*. You may have some favorite principles that you are working on perfecting, and seem to use consistently to actualize your vision into a desired shape or success. For example, I am partial to *congruency, authenticity* and *ethical integrity*. The most important aspect of principles is our ability to articulate and practice their meaning. As are most words, they are open to interpretation. When we want to share meaning with others, the fewer assumptions we make about our common understanding, the greater will be our clarity. This is the same clarity that is helpful when explaining a stitch that someone is admiring in your knitting. It is helpful to know if you are knitting with the left hand or right, how you wrap the yarn between your fingers to maintain the desired tension, and what procedure you are using for passing the stitches from one needle to the other. This kind of practical application is also useful when developing clarity about a particular principle. We each seem to choose principles that are most meaningful to us when actualizing our visions. For the purposes of this discussion, I have chosen only one of these principles that are meaningful to me, rather than embarking on a comprehensive dialogue about each of the various principles we may wish to use.

To explain in practical terms in the principle of *congruency*, Kenneth Cloke and Joan Goldsmith in *The Art of Waking People Up* eloquently describe congruence as:

> a quality of connectedness or unity between our thoughts, feelings, words, tone of voice, body language, facial expressions and actions... When we are congruent, our behaviours match our values, we are honest with ourselves and others, we listen to feedback for indications that we are sending mixed signals, and we are willing to take committed action to avoid creating false impressions (2003:15)

As a pattern of stitches then, *congruency* exists when you can look at the underside of a garment and see how the various coloured yarns have been carried consistently forward to create the pattern on the front. If the practice of using the stitches was incongruent there would likely be a balled up mess on the back of the garment – possibly giving a false impression that the person knitting knew how to use the pattern of stitches skillfully, to create the design on the front. This is frustrating for the person wanting to discover how to repeat the patterns. It was also likely frustrating for the originator of the garment – who perhaps was attempting an unfamiliar design without adequate clarity or experience. What would draw another to look at the back of the garment could be either the even, consistent pattern or the tiny inconsistencies in the design that may not even be readily apparent until we flip the garment over and have a look at the underside. Like the messy underside of a badly knit garment, when we are incongruent we lose credibility, trust and clarity to others.. Our relationships become frustrating and "negotiations turn into a series of 'power plays' and win-lose propositions

with little opportunity for mutually satisfying collaborations and partnerships"
(Cloke & Goldsmith, 2003:15)

In applying a *concept of persistence*, my use of congruency is one of the means by which my vision will take shape or *stand*. I hold the intent of my vision in a similar fashion as the tension on the yarn – ever present, steady – while adjusting as necessary to subtle needs of the pattern I am creating. As a leader I am responsible for articulating a common vision for my organization, team and community – so that the piecing together of the collaborative parts of a garment knit by a variety of people may create our desired result. Or possibly, we will discover we have created something totally knew and unexpected, that may be even more pleasing than could originally have been imagined. The level of common clarity and understanding both internal and external to creating the garment and to the process of knitting, releases the greatest opportunity for success. Discussions, articulation, clarity, and agreement about the vision allow for flexibility in choosing the principles most useful at various stages during the actualization of the vision. The level of persistence with which these principles are applied, connects the original vision with its ultimate transformation into reality.

How might you accomplish your vision?

Focus on holding an even, consistent tension between your intent and your vision, ready to adjust to subtle changes as you proceed. Carefully choose the principles that you will need to apply in a persistent manner. Ask others for their opinion or ideas to assist with your ability to maintain congruency in your efforts. Engage others and build a community of support to accomplish a specific aspect of a vision, and also to enhance the possibility of success for the overall vision. Embrace a belief in abundance and good will – this requires you to acknowledge any small-minded or scarcity thinking in yourself. If you use this approach with persistent intent, then the result seems to take care of itself.

How might you successfully "plan" to reach your goals?

You might choose the vibrant coloured yarn first and then decide what you want to do with it. In practical terms, this means choosing what excites you and then deciding where to go from there – maybe this is where the part of the definition about obstinate – "rarely in neutral or good sense" – is most aptly applied. The intent behind this practice is that it often takes a long time to reach a vision (or knit a complex garment). You might find it most satisfying to begin by working with what makes your eyes dance, and catches your breath – providing deep pleasure just for its own sake.

How might you be happy and optimistic that "things will work out as they should"?

This is about reminding yourself to be detached from your desires. Once you have asked all the questions you can think of, and persistently applied the principles that appear to best fit the situation, then you have done what you can. Will you always be successful in remaining detached? No. You are persistent about reminding yourself to choose detachment – after you have given your best efforts.

Are you nervous about making ten or twenty-year life plans? – What if it doesn't happen?

What if it does? It is the joy of passionately knitting that creates the most beautiful garments, not our fear about how they will turn out.

What is it that might allow you to take great risks and change jobs, career directions, and even intimate relationships?

What if you choose jobs, career directions and intimate relationships based on the principles you apply daily to your living? What if you cannot bear to live less than at your fullest potential, with your abilities fully engaged, and congruent with your day-to-day practice of work, relationships and community? What if this is your ultimate accountability in life? This appears to involve both the act of taking great risks, and the act of embracing others who are on different paths, practicing and persistently engaging different principles. The often unpredictable richness of texture, colour and variety is what makes our visions worth pursuing.

Chapter 3:
Persistence As The Stitches Between Vision And Success

In conclusion, we do not always know what we want to do, nor do we always have a plan, nor are we always sure of ourselves or confident in our attempts. What we can be sure of is that we can give our best and consistently apply a *concept of persistence* to the principles we choose to use. We can engage others in creating shared visions and applying a variety of principles in clarifying, practicing and assessing the results. We can join others in their visions and acknowledge where we can contribute to their success. If we drop a stitch, we can go back and pick it up. If we are unsure of a pattern, we can seek out and ask others who may be able to help. It is the abundance in our shared knowledge that allows for the beginnings of a conversation like the one presented here. I invite you to join me in a continued discussion around what a *concept of persistence* may mean to you.

Coach Farfalla and Jean: persistence – the plan!

Once we have a vision that fills us with possibility – then what? We need a plan. We need a plan that is fluid, responsive and persistently maintains the intent between our vision and actions. Practicing persistence – holding the intent behind our vision and desired success – takes vulnerability and courage. Keeping our thinking and actions clear, sharp and swift requires our full presence in each moment over long periods of time – maybe even a lifetime. We need to notice and celebrate our small successes along the way, building momentum and confidence for ourselves and the community that is engaged in working with us on our vision.

Jean can hardly contain herself. She is ready to move forward and engage her vision. As a senior bureaucrat in the federal government she has often found that it took effort to find her voice and the commitment to accomplish what wasn't always meaningful work. Jean's dedication to the area of her expertise, and a belief in her long-term influence, has allowed for a certain amount of fulfillment as political administrations changed over the years. Now, Jean is beginning her last ten years before retiring with a full pension. Her pension rate goal has already been achieved from her years in various senior positions. There are no particular ladders she wants to climb or milestones to reach in relation to the "doing" part of her career. She has engaged Farfalla to coach her on how to approach her vision for work over the next 10 years, to accomplish what she feels will be a meaningful and exciting achievement.

Jean has met with Farfalla and they have gone through her vision in some detail. The conversation this morning is about how Jean wants to approach the next few months as she steps – or more accurately, leaps – forward.

Farfalla asks, "from our last session, what did you say you wanted to be accountable for accomplishing this week?"

"Well, I went off to research and explore approaches that may be helpful in guiding me over the next part of my adventure."

"Before we begin, can you refresh our conversation about your adventure…. say in a sentence or two?"

Jean pauses and then continues, "Sure. I have been given the lead on a special assignment which mirrors my desire for the future in my field. I am in the position of having a perfect match between my personal vision and the work I am being asked to do over the next five years; in other words, I have just been handed my dream job."

Farfalla laughs softly "I am not sure "handed" is the right word. From what I have seen of your work thus far, you have been pretty good at sharing what you would like to see happen. This allowed others to know when a particular project would be ideal for you."

W hat might be the connection between your vision and your dream job?

H ow does your job re- late to things you love most in life?

"You are right – at times I was likely even a pain about it all! I guess I find it hard to believe that things are finally happening. I am ecstatic and cautious at the same time, which brings me to what I discovered while doing my coaching homework this week. There is lots of great stuff out there, but two pieces of work grabbed me, and left me knowing that I had found what I needed."

63

"Hummm... tell me more"

Jean begins by framing what kind of resources she was searching for. "As I said before, it is not the practical skills of day-to-day leadership that I am searching for. What I want is a philosophical or ideological approach – one that will support tangible attitudes and behaviors for me, and for the team that will be pulled together."

"Umm, I remember that"

"Well, what I have found are two books. The first is a new book by Kenneth Cloke and Joan Goldsmith which is all about being fully engaged and present while working. They call this approach 'the art of waking people up'. It doesn't have all that I need, but it does contain whole sections on such things as sustaining organizational awareness and authenticity. For this project to work, I will need every member on the team to be fully engaged, creative and critically thinking about solutions. Cloke and Goldsmith's stuff is a perfect resource for such a task."

"Sounds like a very good fit, but you said that it doesn't have all that you need. What is missing?"

"I feel that there are assumptions made about the reader's understanding and commitment to purposeful living and work, which brings me to my second treasure. But… I am worried that it may be too flaky or woo-woo for the people I want to recruit."

"What do you mean by 'flaky' and 'woo-woo'?"

"What I mean is that some of the key individuals I need to have on this project are not used to being asked to place their whole self into vulnerable exploration in order accomplish a bureaucratic task. My saving grace will be that I am known for this style of leadership, so they should not be too surprised when I make this kind of request to them, but my biggest challenge is going to be to get that full commitment I want for this project. I am not sure yet how to create the trust and safety we will need to proceed."

Farfalla reflects these observations back to Jean before proceeding. "I can hear that you are committed to an unusual approach for this environment, and at the same time concerned that it may be too big a stretch for some of the people you will need to work with. Can you tell me more about the material you are considering?"

Jean finds herself pausing and then – as usual, leaps forward. "It is Deepak Chopra's *Seven Spiritual Laws of Success*. I am totally in awe of his work, and it is really applicable to this project. This project has such a long history in Canada, and is so loaded with pitfalls and tangles that I feel it is necessary to explore and commit to some of the practices Chopra discusses about approaching history, the future and the present moment. Also, his distinction between intent and desire and the role of detachment is what will provide the foundation we are going to need in order to get the provinces to buy into the project. I am just not sure how to integrate all this into the project."

65

> What would you do if pursuing your vision with persistence meant leaving the security of what you know and do now?

"Can you *hear* the energy in your voice when you are talking?" asks Farfalla.

"Oh, yeah... I have no problem recognizing my total passion and excitement. It is way over the top. I fear someone is going to come along and say 'that's it! She has really lost it this time. Lock her up!'"

Jean waits, trusting that the wait will be worth hearing what Farfalla will offer, knowing from past sessions that Farfalla is taking a moment to step back, to take in the whole picture and context of what Jean has presented to her. Jean knows Farfalla is familiar with Chopra's framing of intent, desire and detachment.

"Jean, I have a suggestion and as always, you can accept, reject or negotiate. Are you interested?"

"Most definitely!"

"I am wondering what it would be like for your team if you fully embodied the principles of intent, desire and detachment in your attitude and actions; allowing the principles to fully influence and express your project without ever naming Chopra's work. This would mean that you Jean, would become the measure and reference point for the principles you want to use. I am thinking out loud right now. Am I being clear?"

"Are you suggesting that I fully own this way of working and represent it as the framework of expectations for approaching the project?"

"Yes, nicely said. That is what I am suggesting. What do you think?"

Jean pauses and then comments "I like the idea, but I am not sure how I will maintain an approach that is new to me for the whole project."

"Hummm, what if you were to add a monitoring method which I like to call 'persistence'? Do you recall that concept?"

"You mean the practice of keeping my eye on where I want to be, and then deciding what the next easiest step is, … doing it, and then reviewing how well it worked… but without knowing what all the steps are to my end goal, and without trying to find a linear path to get there. Is that the "persistence" you are referring to?"

When you have an idea that you are sure is the most ideal approach but it is outside the current culture of your work, what do you do?

"Sure is…I can see it has stuck with some clarity for you! Well?"

"Oh great!" said Jean, with some irony, "now you're suggesting that I own a whole new set of principles, and integrate them into my leadership while not really knowing all the steps that will make that process successful. Is that really what you are suggesting!? This is the project I have been working up to for my whole career, and you're suggesting that I start out with my sails full out, a new crew, new charts and nothing but my good sense to guide me?"

"Yes… along with a solid set of principles that you have clearly said resonate with you, and are appropriate for your project."

W hat is your response when someone asks you to trust and count on your abilities to lead in a new situation?

There is a pause and then Farfalla continues "Would you like me to share what the intent behind this suggestion is, and my confidence in your ability to succeed beyond what you believe is possible at this moment?"

"Please do!"

Farfalla broaches the intention behind her suggestion that Jean herself embody the working principles that Jean would like her team to adopt. "What I am assuming from your comments is that you are not looking for the ability to know Chopra's work, but rather the ability to use the principles he has described, as a foundation for embarking on your project. Is my assumption correct?"

"Yes."

"Can you accept that the best way for us to learn and nurture an approach, is by embracing that approach as an intrinsic part of our way of 'being' in the world?"

"errrr... yes."

"This is the intention behind my request," Farfalla concludes.

Jean's head is buzzing. She feels like Farfalla's words are wrestling with her deepest fear. She wonders aloud: "What if I can't live up to these principles? What if I fail miserably in 'embodying' this way of working?"

Farfalla softly comments back, "and what if you do fail? What if your worst fears come true?"

There is silence as Jean imagines how she might be slain by the lion of her own inadequacy: her career lies in shreds, hanging off her battle-scarred frame. Her prized touchstones of authenticity, congruency and awareness, like emeralds on the sword of her passion, have cut the palm of her own hand, and become tarnished from the streams of self-doubt running down her arm. She has become small, withered and worn. Dragging the sword behind her, she leaves the field of her desires behind and slowly wanders off into a forest full of restless self-criticisms. The branches of self admonishments scrape against her arms and legs, as she admits defeat and surrenders her heart and soul…

In the far distance she can hear Farfalla gently say "Can you let me in?"

As Jean puts words to her imaginary fears, they lose their power and become "just exaggerated imaginings" which leads her to a good laugh, releasing tears of relief and satisfaction.

Jean leaves the call saying to herself "I can do this! ...I do believe it is going to work." She makes a commitment to explore how she is going to use "persistence" to support her, and embody the principles that she has chosen to guide the project. Jean and Farfalla agree on a time the following week for their coaching call.

Two weeks have passed and Jean has had to cancel her coaching time with Farfalla again. She has rescheduled for next week with a commitment to spend some time determining what may be a fully-developed practice of "persistence". At first Jean thought this was an easy task and one that could be done during a few minutes between meetings. Surprisingly, what she has found is that the more she thinks about what a working practice of "persistence" might be, the less confidence she has that she knows what she is trying to define.

If fear and self doubt were set aside, what approach would you like to take towards leading your organization, or leading a particular project?

How can you embrace your worst fears and then provide a catalyst for releasing them? Journal writing, painting wild pictures with your less dominant hand, or throwing rocks into the water are a few ideas to get you started.

The weather has changed. Fall dampness is blanketing the usual morning smell of seaweed and salt. Jean is restless. Fall is a time of new beginnings for her. She has spent most of her life going to school part-time or full-time. But, since completing her PhD a few years ago, the September "back to school" rituals have been by-passed. Jean continues to push against the edges of her resistant brain with no success. She decides to go for a walk and kick the first leaves that cover the path on the trail to the beach. Sometimes, she is forced to accept that giving in to the flow of a day is what is necessary, and that tomorrow will be another opportunity to tackle her challenge. One thing she knows for sure is that "persistence" is not about repeatedly banging her head against her own resistance. Jean will need to push at the edges of her own thinking until the concept becomes part of her whole self and is integrated into her daily actions.

With this truth firmly in place for future reference, Jean heads out to meet that part of her day that is most available to her, and trusts that the rest will work itself out.

Tips for creating your practice of persistence

1. Watch out for "should". If you find yourself thinking or feeling like you "should" do something – change it to an "I will" or "I am" or drop the practice. For example, "By the end of the week I should develop a media campaign for the next six months" can be changed to "By the end of the week I will develop a media campaign for the next six months".

2. Change a "but" to an "and" whenever possible. This creates a connection instead of a full stop between two components of a situation. For example, "I am going to do the funding proposal but first I need to complete the background research" can be changed to "I am going to do the funding proposal and first I need to complete the background research"

3. Continually ask what the intent is of your proposed practice? Does it fit with your vision?

4. Use past success strategies in designing your new practice. When we have found a method that works, it can usually be applied in a different situation.

We often forget to notice what is working and move on to the next task before the accomplishment can refuel our commitment. Keep track of accomplishments – tell people about your small successes and big wins.

Chapter 4

The Multiplicity Of Success

What is success? How might we recognize it when we experience it? Can we agree on its definition? What are the consequences of our definitions? How can we hold ourselves accountable for it? These are the questions that occupy my musings as I begin writing about what I feel is one of the most difficult topics – "success!"

Again, I started with Volume IV of *The Shorter Oxford English Dictionary*, which surprised me in its historical record of how long we have used money or position to define success. The definition begins with "the prosperous achievement of something attempted; the attainment of an object according to one's desire." Then it goes on to say "…now with particular reference to the attainment of wealth or position -1586." A successful person then is one who it obtains wealth or position. The main underlying assumption of the definitions appears to be that 'success' is desirable (and if I may be so bold as to add – at any cost). I find this world-view depressing, dreary, narrow, harmful and self-destructive. For example, how much wealth or fame constitutes success? How much of anything is enough? Who decides? If "we" decide, how do we decide? What values are embedded in a particular measurement of success? How are we accountable for these values, assumptions, and biases?

For the amount of space both literally and intellectually that it currently takes up in our North American reality, success is very poorly analyzed and defined in its specific use. For the purposes of this article I will highlight the multiplicity of success. I will question the validity of ignoring the consequences of success. Finally, I will challenge each of us to consider what we mean when we use the word "success", and how we are living with and measuring the meaning we have given to this word.

We often hear comments such as "their work was a success," or "their life was a success," or "their marriage was a success," or "their parenting was a success," or "their writing or art was a success." Do we all agree and understand that in all of these phrases, "success" is consistently being used in the same manner? – meaning that succeeding in relation to all of those different arenas of work, life, marriage, parenting, writing, and art, is the attainment of wealth and position?

Possibly this is a true definition of "success," but then again maybe we do understand "success" to mean something else. Possibly, since we have come to equate success to be something desirable, we use vague definitions of wealth and position as a kind of shorthand to define its desirability. Hence, by default wealth and position are given primacy in defining and measuring what is desirable. If we can reasonably assign wealth and position to a particular person, then often no further examination of the desirability of their achievements is required. However, in cases where we feel someone is successful, but cannot reasonably attribute wealth and position to that person, then we are faced with explicitly defining why we feel they are successful.

For example, Simone de Beauvoir could possibly be considered a successful writer, philosopher and theorist. With ease we can list her credits for *The Second Sex*; her standing as a central figure in the French Existentialist movement, and her close famous relationship with Jean-Paul Sartre. We are unlikely to question the relentless grueling demands that she placed on herself to write – demands that resulted in frequent cycles of taking wake-up pills, and never sleeping, in order to complete *The Second Sex*, which was written over a two year period (Bair: 1990,392). We are unlikely to question her belief that Sartre's work took priority over her own, and that she was willing to sacrifice her loving relationship with Nelson Algren for her professional companionship with Sartre. We are willing to accept that Simone de Beauvoir is successful, regardless of the high personal demands and sacrifices her "success" entailed.

Another example is a personal mentor I have been honoured to have in my life since childhood. For me his life represents a high measure of success. You will not find his poetry and wisdom in university libraries but you may find it published on the placemats in small restaurants in the region in which he lives. You will not find his wealth ranked amongst the top 25 families in Canada, nor will you even find him given recognition for his wealth within his own small community. His paid career work ranged from jobs such as driving a school bus to janitorial work. His volunteer work ranged from voluntary ambulance attendant to knitting blankets for the hospital auxiliary and the local transition house for women leaving abusive relationships. He does not own his own home or many other material goods.

Are you beginning to question why I feel this individual is successful?

Frank Jordan is successful because he knows how to love. He knows how to love unconditionally and expressively in every day and in every moment. He goes by many endearing nicknames that are used by his whole community, not just his immediate family. To be in conversation with this man is to know your own humble humanity and to walk away hugging yourself – and the whole world at the same time. He has a gift that is rare and valuable. His gift is complete appreciation for life and living. Most recently, we were engaged in conversation as I walked out with him to his car, and he told me how he used his 'little helper' (as he shook the cane used to steady his 83-year-old stride) on days like today – days where he was required to be on his feet for several hours. He told me how blessed he was, because he could still drive during daylight hours. As I stood with him, shivering beside his car, he continued to count his blessings and tell me important stories that he knew I needed to hear. I listened intently, appreciating his calm, confidence as he said "you know god loves me so much that I just can't help myself! I have to spread it around!" His face is lit with the excitement of his conviction, and even from my rather non-committal stance, I would be hard-pressed to deny the existence of his god or his love.

Then with equal importance he continues to tell me how his wife, who is several years older, has not being doing so well. His face is transformed by the sadness of his thoughts. Then he gives his head a little shake and looks up at me before continuing: "most recently she had been having a particularly bad day, and was in tears trying to get dressed, because she was unable at that time to dress or undress herself." At this point in his story, his eyes start to squint with pleasure: "well, I went over and gently helped her, as I laid out my own complaint – I said, 'well woman, you know I love you dearly, and I do not mind helping you take your clothes off at night, but it seems rather cruel to ask me to help you put them back on in the morning!'" He described how her tears gave way to laughter as she called him "an old fool," and blushed from his continued life-long pleasure in her.

His living is an immediate gift, and his stories of living are a continuing gift that offers up a picture of infinite success, in their telling and retelling. Yet, to acknowledge his success (since it fails to fit the acknowledged and typical definition we as a culture have allowed ourselves to accept), it must be carefully and explicitly stated and justified. He has touched and influenced countless lives in his daily practice of joy, recognition and love. I have unquestioning confidence in the huge worth of the rippling effect of his life's work, in giving and receiving. The consequence of his influence in my life alone has allowed me to have hope in the darkest moments, to believe in my abilities, to forgive myself when I fall short of my expectations, and to have total fascination and delight in people and in living. He chose to accept and embrace the paid work available to him, and to excel in using these positions to fulfill his true mission in life, which was to minister to those he met in his everyday interactions.

My challenge for us is to question all measures attributed to success – not just those that are beyond the quick and easy definition provided by wealth and position. I ask that we embrace the multiplicity of success, and carefully explore and articulate what we believe is success in a particular situation, and also what consequences result from that success. For me, success is not about getting it right and sailing to the finish line of life. Success is about allowing your persistence to sail your vision through every day… while the breeze of your passion and potential charts your course.

Determining multiple measures for success

List the aspects that you value most about living. Create a short paragraph describing each aspect on the list. What is the purpose or intent behind each aspect that you have chosen? Be specific about the intent. Specificity around your intent is what allows for creativity and flexibility. For example, you might decide that a sporty little convertible car is part of your measure of success. The intent might be to experience freedom, with the wind in your hair as you are racing along an oceanside freeway. However, if you live on an island, you may decide that a sailboat would be a better measure of your success. Ask yourself how you will know you are successful in each of these areas. At this moment, ask yourself how successful you are in each of these areas.

Coach Farfalla and Katie: success – contextualizing!

Many of the people I have had the pleasure of coaching are women who are very successful in many aspects of their lives, and still they find that they are living with a nagging dissatisfaction. The Coach Farfalla conversation with Katie is dedicated to these brilliant women who have allowed me to step up to their life's work with them – both to acknowledge the success they have already achieved, and to be willing to discover what they might be missing.

Katie had graduated with an English degree and then gone on to pursue training in her area of most pleasure and satisfaction – horticulture. After her parents' death when she was in her mid thirties, she moved back to the small farm of her childhood on the edge of a large urban centre, and began her own business, specializing in herbs and perennial plants. After the first years of struggle, the business has thrived. She has a steady demand for her herbs from some of the fine restaurants and specialty grocers. Katie can count on four or five requests a year to speak at the better garden shows, and she has a column in one of the local papers which gives her consistent exposure and credibility. Mostly, she manages the day to day operations herself, with the addition of seasonal help. Her niece, Jewel, is her main hand, and she works regularly on the farm to support herself while completing a law degree.

Chapter 4:
Coach Farfalla and Katie: success contextualizing!

Katie felt guilty even giving voice to her nagging discontent – discontent that was going to have a negative impact on her business if she didn't get a handle on it. One DOES NOT snap at clients… even if it did seem like a justifiable reason; it wasn't, and she knew that. By most measures, she was a success and so what was she doing messing things up now? Katie had spent the last hour poking with a long stick at her answers to *a few simple questions*. She was finding it difficult to articulate what her dreams were, what she had given up on, and even what was working best right now. When she thought about these questions they irritated her in a similar manner as the patch of Canadian Thistle in the south east corner of her yard.

Katie wonders whether, if she had decided to have children, she would be having this self-inflicted personal crisis right now. She doesn't think so. She enjoys both of her sister's children, and has taken her responsibilities as an Aunt seriously.

"Besides, the right woman just never came along for me to want to settle down." A wiry smile fleetingly appears as Katie teases herself.

Katie picks up the phone, and finds herself continuing where she had left off in her musings, with Farfalla intently listening on the other end of the line.

Following Katie's long commentary provided under a subtext of she-had-nothing-to-complain-about, Farfalla asks, "What dreams have you given up on?"

Katie can't think of a thing, as she stirs the familiar dirt in the same old comfortable, weathered pot that she calls her life and work.

"I don't know," she grumbles, feeling like a nine year old who has been asked what she missed out on getting to do during summer vacation. Her foot even begins to kick at the imaginary gravel at the edge of the road while her rational mind says "don't be ridiculous! You are sitting in your living room!"

Katie cautiously ventures a reply "I have given up on writing. I used to like writing. That is why I did an English degree. Somehow, I have just never made time for it."

When faced with your own success while still wanting more, what can push you to retreat into guilt and inaction? List what you have done to get yourself to move forward.

81

Katie takes a deep breath, brushes her hair back off her face with one sweeping motion before continuing "I have always wanted to tell the everyday stories of gardening. Stories that include the brutal decisiveness that is required when culling plants, thinning, deciding what to grow and not grow, and trying to get the best deal on topsoil or manure. Most garden magazines give the impression of gardening as serene, peaceful work. I find this a myth worth dispelling with humorous tales about the day-to-day challenges I encounter.

Chapter 4:
Coach Farfalla and Katie: success contextualizing!

I believe this would give a much more interesting view of women gardening as they step forward into heavy, hard work that requires ruthless decision-making, skilled use of countless hand and power tools, specific knowledge of biology and chemistry, plus bartering and business finesse.

There is a pause and Katie concludes with a short clipped attempt at humour: "but I have never found the time to write, so we are stuck with serene, peaceful gardening in every magazine lined up along one long isle of the grocery store!"

Farfalla takes a moment and then asks with even acceptance and openness, "what do you think has stopped you from writing these stories?"

Katie begins with exasperation and then gradually begins to reflect on the question Farfalla has asked. "I don't know! Laziness I guess... I just have never got to it... the writing project always felt like it would be just 'feel good fluff' – when there was so much immediate 'real work' to do."

"How would you like to be the one who tells Margaret Atwood that writing is 'feel good fluff' and then ask her when is she going to get busy on some 'real work'?"

Katie starts to laugh uncontrollably at the thought. Farfalla joins her and within minutes they are wiping belly-deep tears from their cheeks, released from acknowledging how delightfully fun we are as human-beings. Katie then began to uproot her beliefs around 'real work' and her desire to write.

If you could change one root-bound belief, what would it be? How would you like it to grow? How does it fit in with the rest of your life's work?

Weeks have turned into a couple of months since Katie's last coaching session with Farfalla – the session where she talked about her desire to write. Her journal has become fat with squiggled seedlings of ideas. The weather mustn't be right because they sure as heck are not growing! Katie muses about where she wants to take her coaching next.

"I was hoping for a quick fix. You know, a headline in the local paper that reads 'Katie fulfills life dream and reclines into bliss.' The more I write, the more aware I am of my restlessness. Like I am missing something, and there is more of that unknown something required, for me to be satisfied with my success."

"hmmm, tell me more…" Farfalla encourages.

"I am not sure there is much more to tell. I have tried all the usual suggestions of imagining my epitaph, or describing what my life is like 20 years from now. None of these seem to be offering any release from this… this tension I am feeling. I suppose it is what is known as a mid-life crisis…"

"Possibly. Can you tell me more about this tension?"

"It is this kind of taut feeling that is both physical and symbolic. I notice it most at the end of the day, and just as I am getting going in the morning."

"Where are you during those times of the day? I mean where are you physically when you get that feeling?"

"In grandma's old chair by the window?" Katie answers with a half question mark caught on her voice.

Farfalla keeps digging "What thoughts are going through your mind at those times of the day?"

"I am usually running through all the things I am behind on, and nagging at myself to pick up the pace."

"Who else in your life may have had this practice?"

"Oh my god! My grandmother! She was such an accomplished woman but she used to sit in that old chair and nag away about what needed to be done, and she never seemed to be satisfied with any of her successes! I don't believe it – I have become my grandmother!" and Katie giggles and slowly shakes her head as she begins to reflect on her new found discovery.

Who has influenced your view of success? List examples of this influence. Which of these are serving you well today?

At the end of their last coaching session, Katie agreed to make a collage wheel that captured her impressions about the success in her life. Katie has been working on this collage about success for the past two weeks. She started with a wheel shape and placed words around the rim, to capture significant elements in her life such as gardening, writing, friends, family, fun, challenge, home, community and so on. She placed a small picture of herself in the middle of the wheel shape. Then she searched for photos, paper, words, cloth, and even leaves that speak to her about her success. Next she used these items to fill the inside sections of the wheel. She still wasn't totally finished, but decided that she had enough completed to have a conversation with Farfalla.

Farfalla began by asking her a series of question such as "What parts of the wheel are overflowing with images?" and "What parts of the wheel have only a few clippings or photos?" and "What part of the wheel is most colourful?" and "What part of the wheel is most bold?" and "What part of the wheel is light or tentative?" and then "What part of the wheel are you drawn too?"

Gradually over the next 20 minutes Katie is able to see how her wheel of success provided a point of reflection on how she defined success and how she was experiencing success. Katie had hated the idea of the exercise because it was time consuming and seemed rather silly. It had been a long time since she had spent her evenings with scissors, glue and magazines. Now she was glad that she had decided to give it a try.

Farfalla interrupts Katie's internal dialogue "What have you learned from this exercise?"

Katie thinks for a moment "Well besides the obvious learning around how I define success and how I relate to that understanding, I am able now to see what is working for me, and what I want to reframe and work on in a new way. But even more than that, I learned that sometimes the shortest route is the least traveled road in the beginning."

"What do you mean by that?" Farfalla inquires.

"Well, I wanted to get to the bottom of my restlessness without having to take the time to explore what was really happening for me. Remember how I thought writing was going to be the answer. After awhile I had to accept that it was a quick fix that gave very short satisfaction before my old restlessness was back with a vengeance. Taking the time to do the collage and really spending time with my life and success gave me greater clarity than I seemed to be able to get just from turning words over. That is what I mean by *the road least traveled.*"

Katie went on to do many wheels in much simpler forms over the next year or two. She published her book about the ruthless side of gardening, started coaching a children's soccer team and began hosting dinners for her friends with seasonal produce from her garden once a month. As a result of her work with Farfalla, what she found was that the "doing" aspect of her success was already well expressed; the source of her restlessness was that she needed and wanted more time "being" with both children and friends – more time in a way that allowed her to offer some of her good fortune and pleasure to others.

Creating a collage wheel of success

A collage wheel is not a tool that everyone will want to use for discovering the multiplicity of their success. Yet, I have found that working with collage can sometimes allow us access to parts of ourselves that we keep carefully edited out of our verbal or written dialogue. The key is to always allow the creator of the collage to interpret the meaning in their own work — by simply being curious and asking open-ended questions. By completing this exercise, you can then ask yourself these open-ended questions with the same level of curiosity about the self discovery.

Time

A Collage Wheel takes time. The process and time spent reflecting on your choices is equally and possibly more important than the final product. Allow between 6-8 hours, preferably over two to three weeks.

Materials

- Large poster board
- A dozen or so magazines that appeal to you
- A selection of felt pens
- Scissors
- Glue stick
- Space on a large surface where your collage can be developed over a couple of weeks

Steps

1. Make a list of the aspects that you identify as part of your success. Some ideas to get you started might be career, family, business, friends, travel, fun, challenge, home, community and so on. The aspects need to be meaningful to you.

2. Take your poster board and make as large a circle as possible on the paper while leaving enough room to write the aspects from your list around the circle.

3. Place a picture of yourself in centre of the circle.

4. Divide the circle up creating a space for each of the aspects of success that you would like to capture.

5. Now begin gluing images, words and bits of information that represents your success for each of the aspects you have identified. The wheel does not need to be filled out evenly — in fact, most often it is not.

Points To Consider

Questions you can ask about your completed collage wheel to assist in discovering more about what success means to you:

- What parts of the wheel are overflowing with images? What might this tell you about yourself?

- What parts of the wheel have only a few clippings or photos? How is this significant to you at this moment?

- What part of the wheel is most colourful and least colourful? Most bold? Light or tentative? What does this mean to you?

- What part of the wheel are you drawn to? What does this tell you?

- What part of the wheel would you like to spend more time on? When would you like to do that?

- What, if anything, surprises you about your collage wheel capturing the multiplicity of your success?

- What would you like to do next? How will you do it? When will you do it? How will you know you are successful? Who will you share your commitment with? How will you celebrate your success?

Chapter 4:
Coach Farfalla and Katie: success contextualizing!

Chapter 5

Understanding Through Representation

The act of leading is not an isolated sandbar unto itself. In particular, women's way of leading involves collaboration and the building of understanding through community. Representation has often been the strategy of choice, and change requires attention to both leading and diversity. Leading in an inclusive collaborative manner needs to be strong and deliberate – pulling and stretching existing social, political and economic structures. Diversity, collaboration and representation often have no relationship, or have only an unstable relationship, with the acts of leading and accountability. Leaders and leading organizations must both lead and address representation with equal and integrated attention.

Himani Bannerji, a Canadian feminist theorist and Professor in the Sociology department at York University, has given a great deal of thought to the concepts of representation and accountability. In her introduction to *Returning the Gaze: Essays on Racism, Feminism and Politics*, she begins by discussing "diversity" and "agency," deploying a notion of agency which goes far beyond civil rights and voluntary participation. Bannerji asks what non-white women are agents for, and where they stand, "particularly with regard to the state and its institutional production of political names or appellations for [them]" (Bannerji, 1993, xxi). I suggest that this is a question that is useful for each of us to ask ourselves when we approach an act of leadership. If representation through agency is understood within a context that "allows" for diversity or difference, then representation is at risk of supporting existing organization structures, structures which support the status quo rather than the development of a more pluralistic society.

Bannerji proposes that such lip-service representation

> seems to be the working out of a political, analytical/
> descriptive apparatus which uncovers the specificity
> of non-white women's oppression while keeping the
> general context and content of capitalism and class in
> view (xxvii).

Present practices of being "sensitive" to difference does not necessarily move decision-making, or create structural shifts, and can actually assist in maintaining privilege and disparities. Sue Findlay, in "Problematizing Privilege: Another look at the Representation of 'Women' in Feminist Practice" uses attempts to undo racism to demonstrate these limitations (Findlay:1996, 207-224). Through analysis of a specific site of struggle at the City of Toronto's Women and Work Institute, Findlay demonstrates that representation can change what is "visible" without changing either policy-making processes or the workforce. Visible changes (whereby the public is served by members from identified "marginal groups" when accessing city hall) are observable – yet close examination identifies that the majority of non-white women are employed in casual, auxiliary positions devoid of decision-making powers. As women leaders, who are often relied on for our ability to collaborate and build community, how might we be accountable for leading with purposeful accountability in relation to the potential risks of such representation?

Transition houses for women and children can provide a practical situation for discussion. These services are a particularly appropriate example for discussing this issue because of the effort, strength and attention these service providers give, to clarifying their contextual environment in relation to diversity and acts of leadership. Yet even from a place of relative strength, representation can still be challenging. A transition house service for "all" women, where the organization has hired non-white women, engaged an aboriginal women's advisory, may *still* find that they maintain decision-making structures, policies and practices that are racist and give privilege to white women. For example, non-white women or women with disabilities may be hired as cleaning staff, to organize donations or as casual on-call shift workers. Women in these positions might then be called on to provide coverage for services during staff meetings, where "everyone's" input is required to make decisions. An aboriginal women's advisory may be consulted for confirmation on the use of healing circles (for both white and aboriginal women accessing the transition house); however, when aboriginal women clients say they cannot find/see themselves represented in the transition house, such comments may be overlooked. Such simple markers as posters, sayings, and pictures of aboriginal people may be missing in a setting where aboriginal women and children make up more than fifty percent of transition house clients. The simple realization that a woman's aunts, sisters, brothers and other extended family may want to stop by to visit while they are in town, does not easily fit with the notion of confidentiality of the transition house location. For the most part, these kinds of issues can be resolved. It would mean changing the way day-to-day business is done and altering the physical environment – possibly outside the immediate comfort zone of the present experience of the organization.

Transition house services are not a unique or isolated site of racist practices. I would like to suggest that these practices are more the norm than an anomaly in feminist/women serving organizations, and are even more

93

prevalent in main-stream society where an analysis of representation may not even have begun. Often these acts of racism – like acts of sexism – are unintended. They are blind spots – missing elements in our design and invisible to us. Leading with awareness about our contextual environment can allow us, without taking offense, to be accountable and deliberate in addressing the unintended consequences of our beliefs and actions.

Findlay also challenges feminists to question the way their practices of representation support privilege. By extension, I would like to propose that this challenge be carried forward as we develop our leadership practices. For example, as a white feminist employed within bureaucracy, I was tasked with regional representation for both government to "all" women and "all" women to government. I have "visible" representation of government through letterhead, business cards, government vehicle and an impressive collection of information. What was not readily apparent was that my responsibility did not bring with it authority for decision-making (commonly known within government as "spending authority") except in a very limited manner. To guide the decisions of government, I attempted to provide regional representation through discussions with (feminist) women's groups and organizations, or individual women. I then was required to present the results of these discussions to decision-makers. Granted, these are not the only forms of representative-knowledge-gathering in governments, but they are by far the most common. The results may be better than no consultation at all, and yet such methods are significantly limited in providing a meaningful contextual direction for policy and program development.

Personal reflection on my own attempts to challenge my view beyond white feminist structures, left me with some disconcerting realizations. My personal connection with diverse women's realities came from women who translate or map their reality onto my experience; they are women who were — fortunately — skilled at bridging the distance between their differences and mainstream white realities. Hence, I did not need to move out of my comfort zone or world view. The only thing that was asked of me was to respectfully listen and then take action as necessary. But at the same time there was little room to articulate what did not fit easily within my immediate understanding. Moreover, in many respects, I was left to work with a translation of an already translated reality, to influence change through seeking the appropriate opportunities, by once again translating these realities – this time translating them into the decision-making framework. (Note also how there are no identifiable individuals, but rather a "framework.")

I also created a bridge for rural/urban understanding for government due to my historical location and trust relations with rural (mostly white) women. Therefore, just as women from other realities map their realities for me, I am skilled at mapping my rural realities for urban (mostly white) women without the need for these women to leave their comfort zone or position of privilege. In fact, in this process of understanding through sensitivity, there is no necessity to question positions of privilege or the structure that continues to support these positions.

So now what? How do we work out an analytical/descriptive apparatus which will uncover non-dominant realities, while keeping the content of privilege in view? Both Bannerji and Findlay look at racism as a fundamental form of social organization in their critique of present practices of representation.

I would like to suggest that the social organization of racism will be useful in beginning to address other socially organized privileges (heterosexism, ageism). I agree with Findlay when she concludes "feminists must seek a vision of society in which our demands for "voice" (i.e. participation that includes power) will not be captured in the forms of "representation" offered to groups today as the way to exercise power in liberal democracies" (1996, 220). Women leaders must face this challenge again and again.

If we are not going to accept the limiting, close-circling movements available within present sanctioned and supported forms of representation, what are the alternatives? This brings me again to Bannerji's notion of re-presentation. If our goal is more than moving the margins to the centre, or seeking representation within present opportunities maintained by privilege, our thinking and acting needs to move beyond these closed-circling understandings. Bannerji suggests:

> by understanding "representation" to mean re-presentation of our realities, from a foundationally critical/revolutionary perspective, there can emerge the possibility of making our very marginality itself the epicentre for change (xix).

Bannerji stresses that "all relations of ruling become more visible where they converge most fully: for example, in the structures of the daily lives of non-white women, particularly if they are working class, and I would add, lesbian" (xix). We can then engage our complex contextual environments in new ways, providing opportunities to image and create changes that are larger than life as we now know it.

How can this change our practices and theoretical positionings, as women leaders? If we start examining our leadership while questioning our perceptions about our lived and historically constructed selves, we can begin assessing our privileges. We can then identify and critically evaluate how these privileges are structurally maintained (and at whose expense). This then provides a framework for accountably engaging with other realities. Our job is not just to be sensitive or to create room for diversity, but rather to engage in revolutionary acts and thinking that can shift structures. Sensitivity is a tool that clears the way for contextual/structural changes, and was never meant to be a gauzy garment worn on the top of existing relations. It is only a thin delicate thread that with skillful handling might be able to carry vision and possibilities forward. Unfortunately, sensitivity is often close-circled as an end goal— sliding off the shoulders of our best intentions into the muck under our feet. Revolutionary acts that view representation as necessary leadership accountability, become an integrated and integral part of our work.

What are the risks of contextual/structural representation? We do not know where our positioning of self will be. We may not like the new accountabilities that we discover, and this is not something we can know in advance. As white women, we may lose our thin grasp on present privileges that white skin and overt heterosexual relationship offers. We may be expelled from the imperial/capital structure of paid work and social acceptance before new structures or ways of organizing are created. Those of us who have spoken and acted out (or observed others so doing) know that the consequences are more than just our fears. They are real. We have heard the comments "there is no appetite for this right now" or "there isn't a window of opportunity". We recognize these as strategic attempts to minimize personal risk (including loss of privilege), while trying to find ways to be heard.

One of the ways to be accountable for our contextual/structural representation is to ask how our agency is going to be used and where we stand in regards to the state and its institutional production. We are then ready to move in a new direction for representation – and this is not an easy task. Our present practices and thinking about representation have become entrenched in state structure (and feminist structures), partly because these practices answer the critique of privileged representation (and, not so obviously, assist in maintaining present structures), and partly because they are the best practices we knew at the time, for creating diversity of voice.

Accountability is not a one-time act but is an activity we must continually repeat anytime we share our understandings and are choosing to act. Donna J. Haraway, Professor of The History of Consciousness at the University of California, challenges us with arguments about the privilege of partial perspective. She argues that feminist objectivity allows for critical positioning, and it is the "split and contradictory self" who can be accountable, "the one who can construct and join rational conversations and fantastic imaginings that change history" (Haraway: 1991, 190-193). Her application is a careful enfolding of imagination, science, research and feminist theory. This may be useful to women's way of leading through contextual/structural representation. For example, in order to act from critical positioning, the subjects or agents of self reveal their vulnerability of location. When desiring to lead with authenticity and accountability would this not be a useful stance? I am intrigued by the dark unsettled watery edges that this concept implies. If we have the courage, we can slice through the current of critical positioning, with each stroke influenced and maintained through rhythmic intent. Differential positioning remains fluid. We can then search for a direction or passage buoyed by what resists simplification in the last instance. Or we can give up – drowned by our own desire for only one assumable objective truth.

Women's way of leading demands that we attend to the challenge of representation. Our historical relationship, as women, to acts of leading, will ensure that contextual/structural representation is integral to our accountability as leaders. We can use our contextual environment as a starting point to begin examining what diverse, collaborative and inclusive practices of leadership need to be developed in a specific situation. The challenge is more than identifying and holding multiple and mobile subject positions. There appears to be a need to pursue named practice and ways of "doing" that create opportunities for change. The subject or agent of self requires concrete opportunities to strategically act from these positions of knowing. A strategy for representation requires not only critical positioning of our understanding, but also critical analysis of the risks for self and others as agents that become identifiable through the exposure of location.

Chapter 4:
Coach Farfalla and Katie: success contextualizing!

Coach Farfalla and Janice: Representation – embrace difference!

One of the great leadership challenges of this time in history will be to find ways to discover and turn over the rich ground of diverse views. There is global pressure to build on the strengths inherent in our differences. The success of small businesses, corporations, governments and countries may well be dependent on their ability to successfully meet this challenge. The following coaching conversation explores some of these challenges from the perspective of a senior bureaucrat in a small country with a diverse population.

Janice starts calculating the time difference on her fingers. Due to travel and meetings, she has changed not only the time, but the date and the place from which she will call Farfalla. They already have half the world between them, and these scheduling changes always increase the chance for error.

Janice had heard about Farfalla's work from a colleague, and since the profession of coaching is still very new to her country, she decided the long distance between them was manageable – and besides, Farfalla seemed to be a perfect match for what she wanted to work on. Janice muses for a moment about being a public servant in a small country where political and economic alliances change faster than the North American preferences for various exotic foods. As Janice dials Farfalla's number, she gathers her thoughts about how she would like to... embrace difference.

After some pleasantries Farfalla starts the coaching conversation "Tell me more about what you mean by this term *embracing differences*."

Before answering the question, Janice begins to outline the context of her work "I think it is important for us to consider the framework within which I am applying my concept of embracing differences. In my country, we have three different populations all working more or less together for the country's survival. We are a poor country by North American standards, but we are rich in community, family, and enjoyment. Desire for socialism, the impacts of colonialism, and capitalistic aspirations have created divisions and contradictions within our value system. As a public servant, I often feel the tension between ideologies and beliefs – not only within my country but within myself. When I think of embracing differences, I want to be able to acknowledge and hold the tension between these positions in a congruent, respectful manner."

The silence hangs for a moment at the end of Janice's mini speech then Farfalla asks "can you give me an example?"

"Let me see... When I am on my way to work in the morning, I stop by the corner juice stand for fresh squeezed orange juice – not because I couldn't have had the same juice at home, or even because the juice at the stand is exceptionally good, but because I know that purchasing this juice is a way to support the people who come from the farms before dawn to set up their stand. This juice stand is their livelihood. When I get to work, I am immersed in public policy about what is government's responsibility to create social supports for its citizens. Data and elaborate calculations (including a formula that is supposed to measure our country's productivity) are used to argue one position or another in order to establish government's role in relation to social policy. I sometimes have a difficult time maintaining my balance in these situations, because the positions are so extreme in one direction or another. I almost feel sea sick trying to find the common horizon line in these discussions and pull together some kind of meaningful recommendation."

Wh)at helps you keep your balance when confronted with divergent views and perspectives?

What are your own positions or beliefs, and how are they affecting your participation in a specific situation?

"How do you see the idea of embracing differences as useful to keeping your balance?"

A week later, Janice is still feeling the ripple of Farfalla's question. Janice mimics Farfalla in her head "'How do you see the idea of embracing differences as useful to keeping your balance?' – What kind of question is that!?" Janice can feel her inner whine of resistance to the question.

Janice twists in her chair as if sitting on a cactus leaf, and begins to doodle on the edge of her paper. She rests one hand under her chin, and bracing her elbow on the table tries to find the words or even a single letter in her brain that she could begin to build around. What was it about embracing differences that she knew, intuitively, holds at least part of the key to succeeding within the tension of her government work? Janice allows the contradictions to scroll down the sparse mindscape of her thoughts. She thinks about how people passionately hold their positions. She notices how their bodies tense with their effort to be understood. She sighs... She is no closer to the answer she wants to be able to provide Farfalla. Her hand finally stills, leaving the last overlapping circle unfinished on a page half-filled with identical shapes.

Janice throws the pencil down, slams her chair back and grabs hold of a light sweater. She decides to head out for a bite to eat hoping that the evening light will provide a cover for the visible lines of frustration she knows are etched above her eyebrows.

> What helps you sustain your position, amid the tension between what may appear to be contradictory perspectives?

"No one said it would be easy" Janice mutters to herself. In fact if it had been easy she would not have called Farfalla in the first place. Janice took pride in her university-educated ability to analyze and deconstruct situations that she came up against. Her time in North American Universities gave her a full command of the English language, yet her heart remained with her homeland. She had been offered other work abroad but knew that what was of most import to her was working in her home country.

Janice sauntered down the narrow street until she came to a rather insignificant little store with two steps lifting it slightly off the tread-worn path of travelers and shoppers alike. Her sister Tina worked side-by-side with her husband to keep the small leather goods store going. She wondered hopefully if her sister will be able to get away for bit. Sometimes in the off-season it was quiet in early evening and they would put a sign in the window that said "back in 10 minutes". Not that this literally meant 10 minutes. It really meant that if it is a birthday gift you are looking for, and you need it today, you may want to try their favorite eating establishment at the end of the street and see if Tina or her husband were there. Of course, if you are not a serious purchaser it would be best if you came back to browse in the morning. But Janice found Tina working inside the store.

Janice and Tina walked easily down the brick street that often had tourists doing nose dives and asking strangers for bandages for their palms and knees. Janice is telling Tina about the question that Farfalla has left for her to work on. Tina nods and listens intently. Though Tina did not offer any solutions, Janice is comforted by the easy companionship that she shares with her sibling. The struggle to find an answer is replaced with discussions about family and friends.

The following week Janice is fully engaged in a one-way conversation with Farfalla. Janice is unfolding an idea: she feels will help her keep her balance when faced with the varied and passionate positions that confront her within the scope of her work. She is talking about her ability to embrace difference – but she has yet to discover how this ability can give her this balance... Janice checks her watch and is startled as she realizes that she has been talking for over ten minutes. She stops.

Farfalla's calming exhale is audible to Janice, who emulates the unspoken request to breathe. Then Farfalla, firmly, with warm conviction, states "I get the feeling you might be circling around your own awareness. Would you like me to check my assumption by asking you a question?"

"Sure, as long as it's not life-threatening or anything." Janice's weak attempt at humour gets the expected serious response from Farfalla.

"No, it is not a life-threatening question – at least, not that I am aware of. However, the power behind this inquiry can alter your world view, and create a shift that does not allow you to return to the place where you are at this moment. This is the reason I have asked your permission before proceeding."

"I see... okay, I'm ready"

Farfalla laughs gently: "first lower your shoulders and exhale! Even over the phone I can see your ears disappearing under your collar in anticipation of what I am going to ask."

Janice exhales through chortles of delight. "How did you know? I sometimes swear that you have special powers!"

What supports you to stand, in the moment of your own discoveries?

Hhow do you keep yourself from taking a risk with your own self-discovery? How do you ask yourself to risk anyway?

Hhow do you maintain the clarity of your discoveries?

"I can't let you know all my secrets! So... what might you be risking in discovering *why* embracing differences is the most desirable approach for your situation?"

"I thought you said I was circling my answer and that I just need to open it up to myself. I don't know the answer to this question any more than the first one you asked me."

Farfalla continues in her gentle firm voice "I am right beside you, standing shoulder to shoulder as we inquire into your questions. I believe you do know the answers and together we can bring them forward. Are you willing to push yourself outside your comfort zone – right over the edge of what you are willing to allow yourself to know at this moment?"

Janice responds affirmatively in a small voice as she feels the fear rise up in her throat. There is a ringing in her ears. She swallows hard, and relaxes her clammy hands as her heart suspends the action of her brain.

She begins to speak without having prepared the words in advance: "I am risking my own sureness of knowing my values and beliefs. If I truly embrace difference, I place my perception on the same plane with other positions. In doing so, I give my view no more or no less importance than other perspectives. The synergy involved in creating an opportunity for embracing difference, is about a willingness to be 'unbalanced'. I must trust that my one way of knowing is truly only one way, rather than 'the way'. In embracing difference, I must surrender to what is, as yet, unknown."

Farfalla and Janice pause long enough for Janice to become fully aware of

What would allow you to release your position into the center of a discussion?

How might you 'balance your wisdom' within un-known possibilities?

her own words – long enough for her to realize that, to gain her balance in welcoming differences, she would need to release her existing position to new possibilities.

"What is it like for you to speak these truths as you know them today – in this moment?"

"I am wondering how I can release my position without losing my clarity and identity. I know now that I recognize that embracing difference is more than being tolerant, more than acceptance. Yet I fear having my way of living and being in the world bullied or subsumed by someone else's perspective, so I hang on tight to my view."

"Humm... Can you now tell me how embracing difference can give you balance?"

Janice changes her position in her chair, leaning forward as if into the center of Farfalla's request, "I intuitively knew that this is what I needed to do. What I was unwilling to admit was that this would require my letting go or releasing my position into the conversation or discussion — and this seems particularly challenging in my work setting. I have huge fear about losing myself if I actually live what I believe will enhance our work."

109

"What would it take for you to be able to take this risk?"

"I need to be able to know that it is safe to be that vulnerable in a particular conversation."

"Can you think of a conversation where you would be willing to consider being that vulnerable?"

Janice mentally races through her 15 projects, and then she goes back over each one more slowly "Yes! I do have one! I am leading a committee on alternative power for rural communities. This is a partnership project between a University, Government, a private mining company and four pilot communities. I sense that there is common commitment to an idea, and yet each person has not clearly articulated their values, beliefs and assumptions. This is leading to an undercurrent in our conversation that is keeping us stuck. The committee's allegiance is high, along with individual ownership. I think that this team would be willing to embrace differences with the intent of gaining balance. Each of us on that committee might be willing to risk placing our individual positions into the centre of the conversation. It would be like believing in and trusting our collective wisdom, while we allow our whole selves, with integrity of intent, to enter into the project. "

If you were going to make distinctions between tolerating, accepting and embracing differences, what would they be? Apply the distinctions in terms of actions toward a specific area of leadership.

Janice's excitement overflows in animated, tumbling possibilities. She appreciates that articulating her new understanding is easier than it is going to be to live and to practice embracing difference. However, she is confident that finding this one situation where she can practice her new understanding, will allow her to walk through her fear. She makes a commitment to bring her idea to the committee. She also makes a commitment to talk to her supervisor about what might be at risk if she places her department's position into the centre of the discussion with other government, private and community partners. In this situation she is willing to take this risk and she knows that other situations will identify themselves. Janice knows the stakes are high. Her credibility and career may be heavily influenced by whether she succeeds or fails. What she is willing to try, is different from how her peers have been working. She also knows that she is willing to grasp the possibility, and act in a way that will provide the team with an opportunity to access their collective wisdom.

Tips for embracing difference

1. Determine what qualities you need, to feel safe enough to release your position into the collective wisdom of a group.

2. Decide what you need to do to ensure those qualities are present and to do it.

3. Put your real and perceived risks on paper. Determine how this information will support or hinder your ability to embrace difference. Ask yourself what it is that you need to do in order to take the necessary risks required to be able to fully embrace difference.

4. Be willing to let others know what you are doing and why. Sharing your goal often creates a greater opportunity for success by strengthening your own clarity in the telling, and by engaging others in your efforts.

Chapter 6

Waking Up To More Than Your Coffee With Unpredicted Change

What is it that unpredicted change has to offer leadership? Opportunity! I have found my greatest learning has come from times when I am slightly off my centre of balance, treading along some high beam, just outside my comfort zone. This is what I call the place of unpredicted change. In hindsight it can be a gift, though in the moment it is often unnerving or even overwhelming. If we compare these times of unpredicted change to a flood – like the sediment that settles after a river rises over its banks and then recedes, these opportunities can provide us with rich fertile ground for growth. If we know where to find what we need to take with us to higher land, if we know how to sandbag what is most important, and if we know who we can count on to help, we have an opportunity to surmount these unforeseen events. Leading in our current global context seems to guarantee opportunities for unpredicted change.

What if we embrace unpredicted change as a gift? What if we believe for a moment that unpredicted change is an opportunity? This is the place where I begin our conversation about unpredicted change.

As human beings, I think that we are drawn to predictability, familiarity and comprehension. For the most part, this allows freedom for the in-between spaces in our lives. For example, I like to know that there is my favorite brand of yogurt and fresh fruit to eat in the morning. This allows me to become occupied with a contract proposal I am writing or a talk I am preparing. There are many things everyday that we simply count on to be as they are. These can range from ideas, material comforts, physical activity, or relationships.

Much research has been done, predominantly on male subjects, in response to unpredicted change. Shelly E. Taylor and Laura Cousino Klein "identified 200 studies of physiological and neuroendocrine responses to an acute experimental stressor, conducted between 1985 and the present, utilizing 14,548 participants, 66% of whom were male" (Taylor Et Al. 2000). Taylor and Klein's latest study, published in the Psychological Review, concludes that female stress response is not exclusively, nor even predominantly, fight-or-flight. In the opening arguments they state:

> We suggest that females respond to stress by nurturing offspring, exhibiting behaviors that protect them from harm and reduce neuroendocrine responses that may compromise off-spring health (the tending pattern), and by befriending, namely, affiliating with social groups to reduce risk. We hypothesize and consider evidence from humans and other species to suggest that females create, maintain, and utilize these social groups, especially relations with other females, to manage stressful conditions. (Taylor Et Al. 2000)

This research is what started my reflection about how we respond to unpredicted change. Taylor and Klein easily navigate the changing currents and deterministic thinking of the nature/nurture argument. By the end of their research, I was left with a clear understanding about the opportunities (in response to unpredicted change) to explore, influence and draw upon abilities and skills. The term "unpredicted change" is a way of creating a distinction in the type of stressor on which I want to focus our attention.

Alas, this issue is far more pervasive than knowing there is yogurt for breakfast. I often wonder how many of us have gone to sleep on the bus-of-work, and have never even noticed when we got on a wrong bus because it seemed like all the others we have caught. How many of us are on our organizational bus and have lost sight of where we are going or how long it will take, and we have long ago got beyond caring who is getting on or off the trip with us? How many of us are driving the bus and are unsure when the last passenger got off, and were surprised when we were asked to close down the run. Our response might be something like "but I have been right on schedule for 675 days! What is the problem?" In these imaginary and not-so-imaginary situations, we can choose to be engaged, and exercise our freedom, or we can choose to switch to auto-pilot, letting the days drag into weeks as we slumber through our lives. Unpredicted change often brings us up short, setting off little red lights and sirens on the mental switchboard of our complacency. We must wake up and drive the bus with full and complete awareness. Whether it is a small item we regularly eat everyday that is missing, or the first news releases about the planes that crashed into the US Trade Centre on Sept 11th 2001, each situation will allow us to wake up to more than our coffee.

I have come to know that I generally take the easiest route known to me when it is time to make a decision. Unpredicted change challenges my ability to know about what is the easiest next step. This has encouraged many wonderful adventures – *after* I have swum through my fear, kicked and stomped out my anger, voiced my disappointment, and finally, reached acceptance about the fact that how I thought things were is not how they are now. As leaders and as participants in change we can anticipate the possibilities for opportunities in these moments. We can consciously build on our understanding of Taylor and Klein's research findings. Who is on this bus with us and how can we support each other? The answer to this question can open up our freedom to focus on the opportunities before us, because we can better anticipate our response to the situation.

Will we have all the answers, making unpredicted change a painless and seamless event? Is there a certain amount of effort that is a prerequisite for engaging with possibility? Sorry: opportunity does not appear to come with any quotas or ratios that will allow us to anticipate the specific effects of our efforts. So whether you are seeking an adventure like the one that has lead 45 year old Linda Cook to become CEO of Shell Canada Ltd on July 1, 2003; or whether you choose to leave your corporate partnership track with a law firm, to write poetry, novels and follow your bliss, as Harvard graduate Tama J. Kieves has done; a measurable level of ease, challenge or personal soul searching are not really a point of pre-event negotiation. The question is more likely to be "are you on the bus or not" or "do you want this adventure or not"? In Kieves' new book *This Time I Dance: Trusting the Journey of Creating the Work You Love,* she shares her moments of misgivings and self-doubt as she questions, and questions again, what she doesn't want, what she does want, and eventually acts on her intuition and creativity. In stark contrast, an interview from July 2003 in the Globe *Report on Business* describes Cook, a petroleum engineer, as "more academic and less fun-loving than her sisters" and having a belief in "never doing anything that makes it obvious that you're a woman or that you might have different challenges than a man." There is no doubt in my mind that both individuals in these separate stories have engaged and managed many moments of unpredicted change, each choosing a path that was right, in that moment and time, for them.

I suggest that there is not a particular path of living and working that is more valid, destructive, exciting, harmful, rewarding or engaging than another. Carol Gallagher, PH.D., in *Going to the Top: A Road Map for Success from America's Leading Women Executives* is clear that though 30% of women managers drop out of the corporate game and choose part-time or entrepreneurial work, her book is for "the other 70 percent of women managers who want to win, who love the power and complexity of big business, and who dream about finding and climbing through windows in the glass ceiling" (2000). In contrast, our evening reading might be *Take Time for Your Life: A personal Coach's 7-step Program for Creating the Life You Want* by Cheryl Richardson, as we sort through what gives us energy, or what drains our desire, vision and dreams. Both directions and perspectives are valid considerations. Often times I find that women leaders hold a taut integrated tension between their career and personal lives. Generally, I find that respect for this tension is not given enough consideration when asking ourselves why more women do not aspire to become Chief Executive Officers or government leaders. We may take solace in a reality check provided by Joanne Thomas Yaccato in *The 80% Minority: Reaching the Real world of Women Consumers,* about how our business world is really not paying attention to women at any level. I am challenging us to know what living-and-working bus we are on, and to be actively engaged in the ride. I am suggesting that we decide our route and pay attention to who is on the journey with us, to where we would like to go, and to anticipate that there will be unexpected opportunities to choose what is right for us again and again.

My request is that we wake up to more than our coffee in the morning; that we breathe deeply, and fully engage with what the day offers and what we offer the day. My heart wants each of us to live each moment fully. My head knows that if we try, we will more times than not succeed. My backbone gives me the courage to make the request and suggest that unpredicted change is a gift of opportunity that we are wise to accept. So whether you are choosing a work-bus or surviving a natural flood along a riverbed, opportunities await.

Coach Farfalla and Rachael:
Unpredictable change – predictable!

Being ready to seize the opportunity of unpredictable change requires reflection, planning and relationship building. To best respond to these opportunities we need to know who we can rely on and who is available to us when our world appears to be in chaos. Rachael examines some of these issues.

It is that predictable time again. Yet, something unpredicted has shaken Rachael's usual confidence, and she is trying to decide how she will maintain her composure enough to articulate the situation to Farfalla. Shifting in her chair she accidentally kicks the garbage container at the edge of her desk. Glowering at her rockports, she grumbles out loud about how someone with an engineering degree should be able to find a functional spot for her own garbage container. Shaking her head, Rachael makes herself comfortable. She firmly tells herself "this is your time and Farfalla is waiting". She dials and as expected Farfalla picks up. Rachael can feel Farfalla's invitation to engage as if she has slipped across the distance via the telephone line. A lopsided grin crosses Rachael's face as she remembers the guest lecture Farfalla gave at last year's Regional Business Conference – a lecture about the 'soft skills' of leadership, stabilized with Farfalla's usual calm persona and conviction.

Chapter 6:
Coach Farfalla and Rachael: unpredictable change - predictable!

Rachael exhales as she launches into their familiar routine. When they come to the question "what do you want to focus on today?" — Rachael hesitates. The controlled air crushing her window-flanked office seems to stagger under the stillness. Rachael can hear the gentle movement of her breath maintaining their connection.

With jagged uncertainty Rachael begins "something has come up and I am having difficulty keeping things in perspective…"

Rachael begins with uneven bits of information about her situation. Gradually Farfalla is able to piece together that the resource-based company where Rachael has been working for a number of years is closing its regional office. There had been anticipation of cut-backs, and possibly shortened work weeks, but a complete closure was unexpected. Due to her leadership position this information had been shared with her as part of the Executive team. Briefings with the rest of the staff were scheduled for later that morning. Rachael will be expected to present the new information in a calm, factual manner, and to provide employees with the best answers available at this time. She is not sure she is up to the task. Rachael has just received the information herself and has not had time to process the situation – part of which is that her own position has been impacted as part of the downsizing.

Farfalla asks, "what do you need most out of your next 20 minutes of coaching time?"

We often are faced with situations that are unexpected. What is your process when confronted with unpredicted change?

What has become tried and true for you in these situations?

Rachael, moves into action mode and responds "I want to review the process I am about to enter with staff and ensure that I have what I need for staff AND what I need for myself."

Farfalla offers, "may I suggest that we start with you first? In my experience, you are meticulously thorough in supporting the people who work with you, which often leaves only what you have left over for your own support."

Rachael laughs, "I hate to admit it but you are so right. Okay, about me.... I don't even know where to begin."

Farfalla gives a short response for Rachel to ponder - "your best guess."

After a few moments and a heavy sigh Rachael admits "what I really need to know is that when this day is over, I can count on my partner to be there to offer unconditional support, no questions asked."

"How can your partner offer unconditional support in a way that will meet your needs?"

121

Rachael responds immediately – "I would like to have Thai food ordered for dinner, a bath run with bubbles, and the evening cleared of all other engagements... plus the ringer turned off on the phone."

"Wow, seems like a pretty clear picture to me. Is there anything you want to add?" asks Farfalla with a soft chortle.

> Quick response teams are made up of people you can count on both inside and outside of work when something unexpected rocks your world. Who is on your personal "quick response team" when faced with the need for high performance under demanding circumstances?
>
> Who can you count on for unconditional support in your personal life?

"No, I don't think so... I will bring the Kleenex," Rachael comes back with a small bit of her usual good-natured humour.

"Well, what are your chances of getting what you need?"

"Pretty good if I ask", Rachael responds.

"So, when are you going to ask?"

"Upon hanging up from our call," Rachael replies, smiling to herself at Farfalla's predictable request for a solid commitment.

"Okay, so is there anything else that you need to support you through today?"

"Are you going to be around at about 3:00, so that we could have a check-in? You are right – I have a process with staff that we use for sharing difficult information, and I have already lined up personnel to attend with me at the various meetings. I need to go back into an Executive meeting at 3:30 and debrief, which is the last thing I want to do. It would be helpful to chat for 10 or 15 minutes just to gather some energy before that meeting."

Rachael can hear the flutter of pages turning.

"I have another client that will take me right up to 3:00, can I call you so that you are not confronted with my voicemail?"

Rachael and Farfalla firm up the details for the afternoon check-in.

Farfalla then asks "At the end of the day, what do you want to be able to say to yourself about how you have managed this situation?"

Rachael thinks for a moment. "I want to be able to say I was clear, and provided as much factual information as possible in a compassionate, calm manner."

"How will you know if you have done that?" Farfalla asks.

"I will be able to look in the mirror and honestly say to myself, it was a tough job and I accomplished it with grace."

What values ground you when faced with unpredicted sweeping change?

How can these values help to provide clarity for your action?

What does it look like when you apply these values?

Farfalla and Rachael close their call with a final confirmation that Farfalla will call Rachael at 3:00 o'clock. Rachael rightly anticipates that this call is an uneventful recapping of her experiences earlier in the day. She accepts that the main purpose of the call is to provide some temporary closure to the events thus far.

By 11:00am the next morning Rachael is just about at the limit of her immediate reserves. Exhaustion is setting in. Her frustration level is high and the last thing she wants to do is take time out for a coaching call. In fact every part of her is screaming rebellion. The company message 'people support what they help create' has become a reverberating mantra on the inside of skull – with little provocation she is likely to projectile vomit. Her day started with an early morning argument with her partner about who was going to pick up their seven-year-old daughter Sarah after work. An optimistic view would reckon that things have steadily declined from there. Rachael would more bluntly suggest that *things have gone to hell in a hand basket and I am not sure if I give a ....* Okay! She chastises herself for going too far down this road of unproductive commentary with herself. Best pick up the phone and get this coaching call over with, so she can move on to the other items that are either smoking or going up in flames on her desk.

"Hi Farfalla, Rachael here and I warn you right now, I am in a miserable mood!"

Rachael imagines Farfalla raising her eyebrows before she asks, "oh, can you tell me a bit more?"

Rachael hardly takes a breath before she launches into a long list of concerns about everything from the direction the company has taken to the fact that she received a parking ticket when she ran in to pick up the her suits from the dry cleaners. After about 10 minutes she stops for a moment, her chest heaving as her lungs rapidly expand for air. Rachael can hear the ringing of her ears in the silence that follows.

After what seems like eternity, Farfalla queries "anything else?"

Rachael is stunned. She doesn't know whether she is going to laugh or cry... maybe both. She was not prepared for Farfalla's simple acknowledgment about what Rachael was experiencing. "I am just not sure I am tough enough for what is ahead and I am so angry. The whole thing seems so unfair. I had my life and career planned. Now it is in a shambles at my feet. Do you think I am losing it?"

"On the contrary, from how you have presented yourself with me today, I would say you are in touch with your experience and how it is impacting you. You seem to be pretty much able to acknowledge that this is a challenging spot to be in — is that accurate?"

Rachael gives a relieved laugh, "I suppose 'a challenging spot' is one way to put it! Yes, that will do." Rachael can feel the tension drain out the bottoms of her feet as she grounds herself to move forward.

How do you respond to unexpected change after the first denial and shock starts to wear off?

What is the process that works best for you to manage resistance and anger?

Three weeks later Rachael is starting to find her way through the immediate impacts associated with closing their regional office. Stiff from exhausting hours cramped into her office, she decides that the meeting room across the hall will be better for her call with Farfalla. Besides, if she leaves the lights off maybe she can vanish for the next forty minutes – one can only hope!

"What I would like to do today is make a decision about the offer the company has made me, to work in Head Office" Rachael says, as she reaches for a print out of the email she had sent on to Farfalla along with her prep form.

"We have about 15 minutes left on this call, how would you like to proceed?"

"Well, I have already outlined the pros and cons of the offer: what it would mean to my life and the life of my family. I am just not sure."

"What part are you not sure about?"

"If I take this offer and we move, what happens if it doesn't work out? I mean here we have the support of family and friends. With this move we would be out there on our own for a while."

"What would you like to do?"

"I would like to go and I am sure that even the goldfish said yes at our family meeting last night. As you know, my partner's work is transportable and Sarah's list of requirements were that she get to bring her new bike, and that her best friend could spend a week with us during summer vacation. It is really me that is hesitating. I love our house. We would have to downsize because things are more expensive out there. I really enjoy being close to family, and we have such great friends here. I also have never thought about being so far away from what is happening in the field. That is always what has given me energy at work."

"What would it take for you to be willing to take this offer?"

"Oh, good question….well, if I could visit the sites I will be responsible for on a regular basis, and I received 20% more than they are offering me now, then maybe we could find a similar place to what we have here. If that were possible, I would jump at the chance. We have been away from family before, and we actually made some long lasting friendships."

"So what are you waiting for?"

"What?"

"If that is what it would take for you to accept the offer, who do you need to talk to?"

Rachael starts to giggle "You know, I did not want to do this call today. I hate negotiating for myself. I can get anything for the Region or clients, but it is so much harder to ask for what I want. And I somehow knew that was what I needed to do. Very good Farfalla! Yes, I will talk to Fred at 3:00. We have a meeting scheduled to go over some other things anyway."

"How will you know you are successful in presenting your offer?"

"As I deliver the offer, I will have a solid, calm feeling in the pit of my stomach and will be able to be relatively detached from the response I receive."

Rachael has made a decision to pursue the offer before her. She knows that she could have just as easily decided that her family, friends and home were her greatest pleasures and went in search of new work in her existing community. Is one decision more true, worthwhile or correct than another? Rachael decides that only for the person who is making the decision does one direction seem to have a stronger calling. She has taken the time to look inward and outward to find out what is right for her. At another time, the answer may be different.

Chapter 6:
Coach Farfalla and Rachael: unpredictable change - predictable!

Conclusion: Hefting the Sword of Gender Analysis

I am becoming increasingly aware of a warped and gaping hole in North American society – between (on the one hand) our society's growing wealth of information about gender-related social realities, and (on the other hand) our continued policies, attitudes, and actions related to gender. To skillfully slice through our resistance we must be willing to pick up the heavy sword of gender analysis with both hands. The inference between individual action with an instrument designed for battle and gender analysis is deliberate and intentional. Gender analysis requires skillful and purposeful practice while we fully acknowledging its strength. To adequately define and explore ways to enhance women's leadership, it seems necessary as leaders to understand and engage in gender analysis. We must practice moving this powerful instrument in precise and graceful arcs. I have chosen three examples out of a wide range of possibilities. In brief:

1. A three hour documentary film *The Corporation* repeatedly allows for an examination of the level or resistance to gender analysis. The psychopathic nature of the corporation appears to have a single-purpose agenda – to make money, at any cost. Yet corporations are not paying attention to the significant financial opportunities pointed out by gender research. It may be to women's benefit to be outside the corporate focus; however, the implication still remains that even if it would increase profits, corporations

131

are unwilling or unable to analyze the gender implications of their business practices.

2. In 2004 in Canada, the British Columbia Liberal government has a deep groove in its audio logo about a "new era for ALL British Columbians" (emphasis mine); however, they provide limited evidence that they are paying attention to better than 51% of the province (women). Women in British Columbia may be just has happy to have the liberals bungle their new era for all. Yet, it remains evident that the liberal approach is negatively affecting women's support for their leadership.

3. Product developers in their marketing efforts have embraced one or a few women as though they were representatives of the entire diverse population of women – of that whole 51% of our society. Again, women may not be interested in seeing gender analysis used in product development. However, products continue to be developed without an analysis of gender implications.

In each of these situations, gender analysis is available and has failed to significantly influence the actions of leaders or improve the results for their organizations in these environments. What is the gap between the available knowledge and the resulting action in these cases?

Despite the "make money" purpose of corporate identity, corporations seem to have been waiting for the 2004 release of research by *Catalyst* (a leading researcher and advisory organization working to advance women in business). In "The Bottom Line: Connecting Corporate Performance and Gender Diversity", *Catalyst's* research on 353 of the *Fortune 500* corporations between 1996 and 2000 showed that:

> Companies with the highest representation of women on their top management teams experienced better financial performance than the group of companies with the lowest women's representation. This finding holds for both financial measures analyzed: Return on Equity (ROE), which is 35.1 percent higher, and Total Return to Shareholders (TRS), which is 34.0 percent higher (*Catalyst*. 2004).

Now if profit is the number one motivator for corporations, I am thinking that long before the release of *Catalyst's* recent research finding, corporations would have been exercising their profit potential through gender diverse leadership. Traditional news and industry e-journals coverage (first 50 sites on a Google search) about these findings does give the impression that corporations have the information and are now paying attention. *Catalyst* reports that "women's representation within *Fortune 500* senior ranks increased from 10.0 percent in 1996 to 15.7 percent in 2002"– we will have to wait to see if there is any further increase in the gender diversity of corporate leadership. What is so surprising in this example is that corporations, which have consistently and single-mindedly re-invented themselves to increase their profits, have also been totally disregarding the positive bottom-line *influence* of gender diversity in the senior levels of their organization.

During its 2001 – 2005 term in office, the Liberal government of British Columbia appears to be bent towards self-destruction in its understanding

Conclusion:
Hefting The Sword Of Gender Analysis

about who makes up "all British Columbians" in the new era. An Ipsos-Reid poll released in March 2004 found 71 percent of women disapproved of Gordon Campbell's performance as Premier (compared to a 57 percent disapproval rating among men who were polled). The Canadian Centre for Policy Alternatives released a research paper about the negative effect of BC government downsizing on women's employment between 2001 and 2004 (Fuller and Stephens: December 2004). Somehow there is a leadership disconnect between gender impacts of government service cuts, and their unpopularity with women voters. To the Premier's credit, he did hire Joanne Thomas Yaccato, a corporate gender lens specialist, to talk to his leadership team. But even after a leadership presentation by Yaccato and a required reading of her book *The 80% Minority: Reaching the Real World of Women Consumers,* by members of his caucus, there seems to be little evidence that our Liberal leaders "get it." When Minister Murray Coell, Minister for Community and Aboriginal and Women's Services, was asked by CBC Radio One on February 6, 2004 about the $1.7 million funding cuts to B.C. women centres, he replied "I think any time you have change, it disrupts some peoples' lives". What the government seems to be missing in this comment is any realization that the "disruption" anticipated might possibly impact their leadership or margin of leadership after the next election in 2005.

The millions of dollars companies spend on product development do not seem to have been spent any more wisely with respect to the real world of women consumers. There seems to be some misconception that if a woman or a few women design a product – then it must be gender sensitive. In March 2004, Volvo introduced the YCC model, touting that it has been designed and developed by women, and features a pink and lavender colour

134

scheme, rosebud cloth seats, and an indent in the head rest for ponytails. I don't know about you, but this does not inspire me to run out and trade in my 1991, F150 Ford, 4X4 pickup. But maybe that is just me. Another example is the woman-designed urinals shaped like a woman's mouth, which the Virgin Atlantic Airways were going to put into their new executive clubhouse at the JFK Airport. According to the company, the red lips, shaped like a puckered-up mouth, were meant to be "fun and quirky." They somehow seemed to think that because the idea came from a woman designer it would be "okay". Just the smallest, tiniest bit of gender analysis may have allowed the company to grasp the misogynist nature of the product, and to anticipate and avoid the public outcries which embarrassed them and shamed them into a new design.

What will it take for gender analysis to become an everyday practice, as normal as brushing our teeth? We have the information that tells us what we are failing to do, that would help us to avoid creating serious social cavities – the gaping social holes I have been talking about. How can we encourage the regular practice of simply 'having a look and acting on' gender implications – in relation to everything from our financial agendas, our governance, to the creation of the products we produce? In discussing women's leadership, gender analysis becomes a significant factor for explicitly defining a particular contextual environment. It takes training, practice and discipline to heft the sword of gender analysis, but the extent to which we can enhance our acts of leadership make it worth the effort.

Women's ways of leading are necessary in every leadership arena. These are ways of leading that value collaboration, diversity and inclusive practice.

135

Conclusion:
Hefting The Sword Of Gender Analysis

These acts of leading are authentic, accountable and practiced with vulnerable integrity. We may not want corporations to make money from women's leadership abilities. We may not want the Liberal Government of British Columbia Canada to find a way to attract women's votes. And, we may not care about urinals. Regardless of what we may want or care about, these situations negatively impact women. These situations are examples about aspects of our contextual environment that influence our leadership practice. We have an opportunity to ask ourselves about how we might influence, change or lead our society in a new way. We can ask ourselves how we might be supported in our leadership. Women have agency. We can and will use it with graceful purposeful intent.

Bibliography

Anderson, Kathy. 2003.
Personal Best Consulting and Executive Coaching Services
www.dentalcoaching.ca

Anzaldúa, Gloria. 1987.
Borderlands/LA Frontera: The New Mestiza
San Francisco, CA. Aunt Lute Book Company

Bannerji, Himani. 1993.
Returning the Gaze: Essays on Racism, Feminism and Politics
Toronto. Sister Vision Press

Bair, Deidre. 1990
Simone de Beauvoir: A Biography
Summit Books. New York

BC Coalition of Women's Centres. 2004.
"Making Jam 2004: Stop The Deaths of BC Women's Centres!"
http://www3.telus.net/bcwomen/eulogy/

Butler, Judith. 1990.
Gender Trouble: Feminism and the subversion of identity
Routledge. New York

Catalyst. 2004.
"The Bottom Line: Connecting Corporate Performance and Gender Diversity"
Catalyst, New York, San Jose and Toronto
http://www.catalystwomen.org/knowledge/titles/files/exe/fpexe.pdf

Cooper Peter. J. April 15, 2003.
AME INFO FN Middle East Finance and Economy: Executive Interview
http://www.ameinfo.com/news/Detailed/20201.html

Bibliography

Cloke, Kenneth & Joan Goldsmith. 2003.
The Art of Waking People Up: Cultivating Awareness and Authenticity at Work
San Francisco, CA. Jossey – Bass

Crnkovich, Mary. 1990.
GOSSIP: A Spoken History of Women in the North
Ottawa. Canadian Arctic Resources Committee. Canada

De Beauvoir, Simone. 1952.
The Second Sex. Translated and edited by H.M. Parshely
Vintage Books. New York

Findlay, Sue. 1993.
"Problematizing Privilege: Another look at the Representation of "Women" in Feminist Practice"
and
in And Still We Rise: Feminist Political Mobilizing in Contemporary Canada, edited by Linda Carty, 207-224
Toronto, Canada. Women's Press.

Fuller, Silvia & Lindsay Stephens. 2004.
"Women's Employment in BC: Effects of Government Downsizing and Employment Policy Changes 2001 – 2004"
http://www.policyalternatives.ca/documents/BC_Office_Pubs/women_employment_bc.pdf

Gallagher, Carol, PH.D., with Susan K. Golant, M.A. 2000.
Going to the Top: A Road Map for Success from America's Leading Women Executives
Penguin Group, USA

Hamilton, Roberta. 1996.
Gendering the Vertical Mosaic: Feminist perspectives on Canadian Society
Hamilton, Copp Clark Ltd, Toronto

Haraway, Donna J.. 1991.
Simians, Cyborgs, and Women: The Reinvention of Nature
Routlege, New York

Kieves, Tama J. 2003.
This Time I Dance: Trusting The Journey of Creating The Work You Love
Penguin Group, New York, USA

Laundry, Donna & Gerald Maclean. 1993.
Materialist Feminisms
Blackwell Publishers, Cambridge, Massachusetts

Onions, C.T., Editor. March 1933.
The Shorter Oxford English Dictionary on Historical Principles, Volume III
Oxford University Press, London

O'Neill, Mary Beth. 2000.
Executive Coaching with Backbone and Heart: A Systems Approach to Engaging Leaders with Their Challenge
Jossey-Bass: A Wiley Company. San Francisco, CA

Richardson, Cheryl. 1999.
Take Time for Your Life: A Personal Coach's Seven-Step Program for Creating the Life You Want
Broadway Books, New York

Bibliography

Scottsdale National Gender Institute. 2003.
The Business Case for Gender Diversity Phoenix.
http://www.gendertraining.com/Business%20Case%20for%20Gender%20Diversity.pdf

Smith, Dorothy E. 1990.
The Conceptual Practices of Power
University of Toronto Press. Canada

Taifour, Majed G. September 2003.
"Greater Equality for Women Sought in United Arab Emirates"
Choices: The Human Development Magazine
http://www.undp.org/dpa/choices/2003/september/uae.html

Taylor, Shelly E., Laura Cousino Klein, Brian P. Lewis, Tara L. Gruenewald,
Regan A. R. Gurung, and John A. Updegraff. 2000
"Biobehavioral Responses to Stress in Females: Tend and Befriend, Not Fight-or-Flight"
in *Psychological Review* Vol. 107, No. 3, 411-429

United Nations. Rev.3 27 January 2004.
Excerpts from The World's Women 2000: Trends and Statistics
http://unstats.un.org/unsd/demographic/ww2000/index.htm

US Basic Income Guarantee
NEWSLETTER VOL. 5, NO. 25, JANUARY-FEBRUARY 2004
http://victoria.indymedia.org/news/2004/02/22185.php

Walmsley, Ann.
"Introducing Linda Cook"
in *Report on Business,* The Globe and Mail, June 27, 2003, 26 ff.

Weedon, Chris. 1987.
Feminist Practice & Postructuralist Theory
Basil Blackwell Inc, New York.

Wheeler, Charlene Eldridge & Peggy L. Chinn. 1991.
Peace and Power: A Handbook of Feminist Process
National League for Nursing Press. New York

Womankind Worldwide: Creating A Difference. 2003
http://www.womankind.org.uk/about%20us/faq.html

Wright, Susan & Carol macKinnon. 2003
Leadership Alchemy: The Magic of The Leader Coach
The Coaching Projects Publications, Phoenix, Toronto and Vancouver

Yaccato, Joanne Thomas with Judy Jaeger. 2003.
The 80% Minority: Reaching the Real World of Women Consumer
Penguin Group, Canada

Bibliography

More About Terrill Welch – A Woman Behind Women

Terrill Welch's life-long learning objective is to facilitate social change through action-oriented opportunities. Her work is designed and delivered specifically to meet the needs of women with leadership responsibilities locally, nationally and internationally. She provides leadership and coaching services that attract women leaders and organizations seeking a holistic and integrated approach to achieving success.

Terrill's academic background includes a degree in Sociology and Women Studies; certification in Graduate Executive Coaching, and in Public Sector Leadership from Royal Roads University; a master's degree in Gender Studies is in progress. Terrill has years of experience in using a coach approach with employees, peers, clients, and in organizational team development. This is combined with almost as many years' experience in various leadership positions, including Director of the Stopping the Violence and Regional Programs Branch, for the former British Columbia Ministry of Women's Equality. She is a past President of the International Coach Federation's Vancouver chapter. In December 2004, she became the Executive Director of the Women's Resource Society of the Fraser Valley, a large agency serving the needs of women; which contracted with her to provide both leadership and coaching services in order to develop and implement their strategic direction. These endeavors ensure that her leadership theories and practices are continually being applied and refined.

Leading Raspberry Jam Visions: Women's Way is Terrill Welch's second book. Terrill is also the author of a handbook entitled *Process to Protocols in Response to Violence Against Women in Relationships,* published in 1994. That publication has been a resource for communities to develop protocols in communities throughout British Columbia, across Canada and as far away as New Zealand.

Terrill is a leader, feminist, writer, artist, mother, grandmother, partner and friend who is passionate about creating a world she wants to live in. She credits the diverse perspectives of her parents for giving her the ability to successfully engage in such rich possibilities. Her father's good-natured laughter and love of work combined with her mother's no-nonsense approach to most situations was just the foundation Terrill needed. She laughs and cries with the greatest of ease and lives life with large amounts of energy and quiet contentment. An executive coaching client recently commented, "She is this extraordinary powerhouse of a woman wrapped up in the most gentle of spirits".

Keynote Speaker, Consultant, Executive Leadership Coach
For more information: www.awomanbehindwomen.ca

Notes

Notes

Notes

ISBN 1-41205961-5